DAN TOOMBS

THE CURRY GUY BBQ

100 Classic Dishes to Cook over Fire or on Your Barbecue

Photography by Kris Kirkham

Hardie Grant

QUADRILLE

CONTENTS

PREFACE

Cooking over fire has played a big part in my life. I have so many fantastic memories of get-togethers with family and friends, standing around a campfire or barbecue and cooking up a feast. There are few things better than bringing together a group of people to enjoy delicious food.

My earlier cookbooks all feature a barbecue section, but I wanted to take things further and include recipes that you might not have considered for a weekend barbecue, which is why I decided to write this book.

When most people think of a barbecue, they picture a kettle-style barbecue that can be used for both indirect and direct heat cooking. If you have one, you will be able to make the majority of the recipes in this book but I have also included recipes that go beyond the standard barbecue set-up; these recipes can most often be tailored to the barbecue you have or a campfire.

Nowadays, it's easy to forget that in the not-so-distant past, all cooking was done either over fire outdoors or with a wood-fuelled oven indoors. I can still remember going to my great-grandmother's house and watching her light up her wood-burning stove to cook dinner. What was once a daily chore for our ancestors is now something we look forward to as a weekend activity.

I mention this because everything you can cook inside in a modern kitchen can be cooked outside, too. Cooking outdoors with wood or charcoal can be a lot of fun and personally I think the food tastes better as well. That's right... curries, tandoori recipes and even fried and steamed foods taste better when cooked over a live fire, just as they are all over the Indian subcontinent and at restaurants and food stalls here in the West.

I have been so inspired by street-food vendors and chefs who have opened their kitchens to me, both in the UK and abroad.

Watching them cook roasts, skewered meats, paneer, vegetables and even frying over a log or charcoal fire made me want to do this at home. Knowing that many readers of my cookbooks like a good curry-house-style curry, I've included a section on cooking these on the barbecue.

At my house, we barbecue year-round. Even our Christmas turkey is cooked on the barbecue, regardless of the weather, and these recipes are far too good to be seasonal! For this reason, I have provided cooking temperatures where possible, as well as the internal temperatures you should be aiming for (after all, barbecuing is all about cooking to temperature, not time), which can be followed whether you are cooking outside on the barbecue or inside using an oven.

It was important to me that these recipes remain simple and authentic to their origins. At times this was tricky. Burying a whole chicken wrapped in banana leaves in a pit of red-hot charcoal to cook for a couple of hours isn't something most people are going to be able to try. Recipes that are traditionally cooked in a tandoor oven would be of little use to those who don't have one. With this in mind I have kept the recipes simple and without the need to dig any holes or run out to purchase a tandoor.

If you have any questions about the recipes in this book, please get in touch through my social media channels. Getting to know the people who read my books is one of the things I enjoy most about writing them. I'm @TheCurryGuy on Twitter, Facebook and Instagram and I'd love to hear from you. You might also like to join my Facebook group, Curry Chit Chaat. It's a great community and I'm almost always on hand to answer questions.

Happy Cooking!

GETTING STARTED

To help you find the recipes you might like to try, I have labelled them with these badges.

 Gluten-free: The good news for people that need to stick to a gluten-free diet is that most of my recipes are naturally gluten-free.

 Vegetarian: Look for this badge to find some of my favourite vegetarian recipes. Most of the sauces in the British Indian Restaurant-style chapter are also vegan; others can be made so by switching to non-dairy alternatives.

 30 minutes or less: Look for this badge if you want to prepare something quickly. However, this does not include the time it takes to light your barbecue, or passive preparation such as chilling or marinating or making any special marinades or pastes.

 Direct heat: This badge indicates that a recipe is cooked directly over the coals of your barbecue. This is grilling and it's the easiest method for outdoor cooking. You will find more information on cooking over direct heat opposite.

 Indirect heat: You will need a barbecue with a lid to cook over indirect heat. This cooking method is used for smoking, barbecuing and roasting. For more on cooking over indirect heat, see opposite.

BARBECUES AND GRILLS

No matter what size your barbecue is, the principle is always the same: fuel, fire and oxygen create heat. Adjusting the amount of fuel you use and the amount of oxygen that gets to your fire will determine how hot it is. It's really that simple. But when you are just starting out, you will need to get to know your barbecue and how best to use it.

Below is a breakdown of the most popular types of barbecue and grill on the market. If you have a kettle or ceramic barbecue, you'll be able to cook pretty much every recipe. If all you have is a small grill without a hood, you'll find plenty of recipes you can make with that, too.

KETTLE BARBECUES
Almost everyone will recognize the Weber kettle barbecue, as it has been the most popular barbecue for home cooks for decades. These barbecues are affordable and are great for both direct and indirect heat cooking (see opposite).

CERAMIC BARBECUES
Ceramic barbecues are all the rage now, and for good reason: they offer a cooking experience that is far superior to the standard kettle barbecue. I love my Kamado Joe. These barbecues are built with ceramic materials, which means you get a more even cook, because the ceramic interior heats up and radiates that heat from all sides like a tandoor, unlike standard metal kettle barbecues, which cook mainly from the bottom. Ceramic barbecues also heat up much faster and to hotter temperatures than other barbecues and maintain your preferred cooking heat more easily. What's more, if you need to lift the lid to baste meat, the barbecue won't cool down. It will get back up to heat in no time because of the hot ceramic.

Another bonus with ceramic barbecues is that there is no need to place a drip pan of water in it when cooking over indirect heat, other than to keep the barbecue clean.

GRILLING AND SKEWER BARBECUES

Anyone who follows my blog will know that I am also a big fan of THÜROS tabletop grills and their kebab attachments. These are excellent for preparing food over direct heat. For larger, more elaborate cooks, I love the Kadai Firebowl pictured on page 68!

SMOKE PELLET BARBECUES

These fantastic barbecues are fuelled with small wood pellets that feed the fire and give off a great smoky flavour. The most popular ones are made by Traeger and couldn't be easier to use. Pellet barbecues are perfect for indirect roasting and barbecuing – while you have to watch the cooking temperature of kettle and ceramic barbecues carefully, with pellet grills you can simply set the temperature you require, place whatever it is you're roasting or barbecuing on the rack and leave it to do its job. On the downside, they aren't great for searing and other direct heat cooking, but a small tabletop grill along with your pellet grill will solve that issue.

GAS BARBECUES

I'm not a big fan. I cooked on a gas barbecue for years, but much prefer cooking over live fire. However, gas does make it easy to regulate the cooking temperature and you can still achieve a nice smoky flavour by adding soaked wood chunks while cooking.

TANDOOR OVENS

Outdoor tandoor ovens are becoming more and more popular and are about the same price as a good gas or wood-burning barbecue. Many of the recipes in this book can be cooked in a tandoor; if you have one, do check out the tandoor oven basics information on my website: https://greatcurryrecipes.net/how-to-use-a-tandoor-oven/

COOKING TECHNIQUES

There are six techniques for cooking with fire: cold smoking, hot smoking, barbecuing, roasting, grilling and cooking in the embers. Of these, only the last four are used in this book.

BARBECUING (INDIRECT HEAT)

Although we might call that piece of cooking equipment in our garden a barbecue, 'barbecuing' is in fact a cooking technique that was developed to cook large and/or tough cuts of meat such as beef brisket, pork butt and racks of ribs, which need to be cooked low and slow to become tender. Traditional barbecuing is done over indirect heat at temperatures between 82°C (180°F) and 125°C (257°F). Unlike other cooking techniques, with barbecuing, 'doneness' is not determined by the internal temperature of the meat but by its falling-apart, mouth-watering tenderness. There will normally be an internal temperature to aim for (and I have provided these).

ROASTING (INDIRECT HEAT)

For roasting, you are aiming for a temperature between 180°C (355°F) and 260°C (500°F). Roasting on a barbecue is just like roasting in your home oven, but in a smoky environment. Meats that you might expect to cook at these temperatures are whole chicken, duck or turkey, or even fillet of beef. It's really important to check the internal temperature before serving – to make sure it's done, but for the beef fillet especially, to check that it's not overcooked.

GRILLING (DIRECT HEAT)

Grilling is the simplest and most popular way of cooking outdoors. It can be done on pretty much any barbecue, or on a campfire, and is just cooking directly over hot coals. There are many uses for this technique, from chargrilling kebabs to frying steaks in a skillet or cooking pork chops directly on the grill. This method can even be used for cooking curries and deep-frying.

When grilling, the cooking temperature can be checked by hand. Most of the grilled recipes in this book are cooked over a high heat. If you hold your hand 5cm (2in) over the grate and it becomes uncomfortably hot after 2 seconds, you've got high heat and are ready to go. Where a lower cooking heat is preferable, I'll explain how to check the temperature in the individual recipes.

It is a good idea to build a multi-level fire when cooking over direct heat (see page 10). This way, you will have a high heat to cook your food on and a cooler area where you can move what you're cooking when needed.

COOKING IN THE EMBERS (DIRECT HEAT)

This is very similar to grilling, but you cook right on top of the hot embers. Steaks cooked on hot coals take on an amazing char and vegetables can be cooked in this way too, as can curries like the champaran mutton handi on page 112. To cook on the embers, you will usually need a lot of coals. If you cook a steak directly on the embers, for example, it will begin to smother the fire as it cooks. So if you are cooking a few steaks, you will need a large enough cooking area so that when you turn them, you have fresh hot coals to move them to.

LIGHTING YOUR FIRE

Like most people, I used to just squirt a large amount of liquid fire starter onto my charcoal and then throw a lit match at it, happily standing back to watch it burst into flames. Don't do that. You will taste it in your food and that would be a shame, having worked so hard to make it taste incredible.

These days I light my fire using the following two methods.

THE STACK

Anyone who has lit a campfire or indoor fireplace will be familiar with this method. To do it, you will need some way of getting the fire going. Scrunch up some newspaper and place a bit of kindling wood on top and light it. You could also use a natural fire starter or two. Then, stack more kindling and lumpwood charcoal, kiln-dried logs or charcoal briquettes on top, ensuring that everything is loosely stacked into a pyramid shape to allow air to flow upwards and keep the fire going. From experience, you will need to allow yourself a good 30 minutes to get the fire ready for cooking.

CHIMNEY STARTER

Chimney starters are available online and at most shops that sell barbecues. A chimney starter reduces the fuss of building a good fire; it is a metal cylinder that has a large space at the top for loading your charcoal and a smaller space at the bottom that you fill with crunched up newspaper and fire starters. Light the bottom and let the chimney do its job. In about 20–30 minutes, you will have a full chimney of lit charcoal ready to use. However, you'll still need to decide how much charcoal you need and how to arrange it for the job in hand.

WHICH FUEL TO USE AND HOW MUCH?

I think of the charcoal and wood that I use for cooking as ingredients in their own right. Good-quality lumpwood charcoal, compressed briquettes and/or kiln-dried wood can add delicious flavour to your food, while poor-quality charcoal will do the opposite. The charcoal and/or wood you use is important. Not only do you want to consider the quality, but different types of charcoal are better for different cooking methods.

Lumpwood charcoal burns hot and fast and adds amazing flavour. I use lumpwood for fast, direct heat cooks. It's perfect for cooking seekh kebabs and other small cuts of meat, on which you want a nice char.

How much charcoal you need will be down to the barbecue you are using and how much food you intend to cook. I suggest using a lot until you are familiar with what works best for your grill. If all you're doing is cooking up a couple of chicken skewers on a small tabletop barbecue, you might get away with just filling up a chimney starter and using that charcoal to cook them. It's very likely, however, that you will need double or triple that amount most of the time, or much more if you are serving a crowd and cooking lots of skewers over a few hours.

The most frustrating thing when cooking outdoors is running out of heat. To combat this, I pour lots of lumpwood into my barbecue and then add burning charcoal from a chimney starter. I give it all a light mix and then leave it to come up to the required heat. If I am doing a long cook, I also fill the chimney starter with more charcoal and light it midway through, so that I have more hot coals ready to add when needed. Adding unlit charcoal to a hot, direct heat fire will just slow things down.

I use about 1.5kg (3lb 5oz) lumpwood to cook 1kg (2lb 4oz) meat but you really need to experiment with your own equipment.

Charcoal briquettes burn at a medium heat and much slower than lumpwood charcoal. This doesn't mean that you can't use briquettes for fast, high-heat cooking, but they are much better suited to slower, low- to medium-heat cooks. They are the perfect fuel for indirect heat barbecuing and roasting. I do still recommend adding more than you might think you need, but you can be confident that they will burn for a good 4 hours, or even longer. Briquettes offer about twice the burn time as lumpwood.

I use roughly 1kg (2lb 4oz) charcoal briquettes per 1kg (2lb 4oz) meat. When I'm planning on roasting for an hour or more, I use the equivalent of at least two full chimney starters, but again, this will vary depending on your kit. At the end of the day, if you add too much charcoal and your barbecue becomes too hot for purpose, you can adjust the heat by allowing less air to flow in and out until you have the perfect heat for cooking.

I love using kiln-dried logs, whether cooking on a campfire or on my barbecue. I use a variety of different woods such as oak for red meats and sausages, apple for slow-cooked chicken, pork and feathered game, and hickory for pretty much any slow cook.

PREPARING A FIRE FOR INDIRECT HEAT

Indirect heat is used for barbecuing and roasting. There are a number of ways to prepare your fire for indirect cooking, but the most common is to pile all your hot coals in the centre to get them started and then shift them all to one side of the barbecue, leaving the other side without any coals. If you are preparing for a long cook, it's a good idea to place plenty of unlit coals next to the lit coals on the hot side of the barbecue. As the fire burns, the unlit coals will gradually light and sustain the required heat.

Another popular way of arranging your coals for indirect cooking is to divide them; push half of the burning coals to one side and the rest to the other side of your barbecue, leaving a cool area in the centre.

Whichever method you choose, you will need a drip pan with a little water in it to place below where you are cooking the meat. This not only keeps your barbecue clean, but the steam from the water assists in the cook. Drip pans are not necessary if you are using a ceramic barbecue; the closed barbecue is naturally moist due to its construction.

When barbecuing and roasting, you will need to aim for a preferred cooking heat. As already mentioned, starting and maintaining a healthy fire is down to your fuel and the amount of air that is allowed to flow in and keep it burning. In a standard kettle or ceramic barbecue this is done by maintaining the amount of charcoal that is burning and adjusting the top and bottom air vents.

For low and slow cooking, limit the air flow into the barbecue by semi-closing the bottom vent. Leave the top vent open until you get the barbecue up to temperature. When almost up to heat, start adjusting the top vent by closing it a little. Do all the fine-tuning using the top vent.

For roasting chickens, beef or anything you would cook at higher temperatures in an oven, open the bottom and top vents fully. This will provide enough airflow to get to the temperatures required. After you have got the barbecue up to temperature, close the bottom vent about halfway, or a little more. You can fine-tune the heat by adjusting the top vent throughout the cook.

Don't waste that charcoal! When you're finished cooking, close both vents. This will suffocate the fire. Whatever charcoal is left can be used to burn another day.

PREPARING A FIRE FOR DIRECT HEAT

Direct heat is used for all sorts of cooking, from grilling on a grate over coals to cooking directly on the burning embers. It is also used for cooking curries, pan-frying and even deep-frying. Think of this style of cooking as you would your kitchen hob. It's used to cook food from below over high, medium or low heat. It can also be used to smoke and cook food slowly, as for the hanging smoked leg of lamb and spicy whole chicken on a skewer (see pages 69 and 55).

You will need to build your fire differently depending on what you are planning to cook. If you have access to a large cooking area such as a Kettle barbecue or campfire, it is a good idea to build a large, multi-level fire. To do this, build your fire as explained on page 8; when the coals have ashed over and are really hot, use most of them to form a mound. This will be the hottest part of the fire, which works in a similar way to having your hob burner on high. The remaining coals can be piled up at different levels to provide cooler areas on your grill where you can move cooked ingredients as required so that they don't burn.

BARBECUE DOS AND DON'TS

Cooking outdoors is really fun but can be a bit daunting if you're new to it. Keep the following DOs and DON'Ts in mind and you'll be cooking like a pro in no time.

DO allow yourself plenty of time to get your fire started. Cooking with fire takes time and you will have a lot more fun and a more successful cooking experience if you take the time to get it right from the beginning.

DO use high-quality lumpwood charcoal, briquettes and/or kiln-dried wood.

DO plan your fire for the job in hand. Choose the right fuel and be sure to have more fuel at the ready to add to the fire when required.

DON'T use substandard, quick-light charcoal, petroleum-based fire starters or those small, instant lighting disposable 'barbecues'.

DON'T add unlit charcoal briquettes or lumpwood to a dying fire; instead use a chimney starter or build a stack fire and then add the burning coals to your fire.

DON'T get frustrated! If you are a seasoned outdoor cook, you will find the recipes in this book easy. If not, plan on getting to know your barbecue. Learn how the charcoal you use burns in it and adjust as needed.

EQUIPMENT

I have picked up a lot of stuff along the way, but I still try to keep things simple and work with what is available. Below is a list of equipment that you might want to invest in to take your barbecuing to the next level.

Spice grinder and/or pestle and mortar
Meat thermometer
Large cast-iron karahi
Small fireproof frying pans (skillets)
Clay handi (cooking pot)
Stainless-steel balti bowls
Food processor or blender
Good chef's knife
Metal skewers
Wire mesh spoon
Barbecue foil drip pans (for use with
  kettle-style barbecues)

INGREDIENTS

I am often asked which ingredients you need to stock up on to get started. I recommend looking at a few recipes you would like to start with and stocking up on those ingredients – you can then build from there. That being said, there are some ingredients that I always have on hand. You can purchase all of these ingredients, but I have given page references for spice blend recipes that feature in this book.

SPICE BLENDS
Mixed powder (see page 132)
Tandoori masala (see page 167)
Garam masala (see page 168)
Chaat masala (see page 168)

FRESH OR FROZEN INGREDIENTS
Ginger
Garlic
Green bird's eye chillies
Fresh coriander (cilantro)
Fresh or frozen curry leaves (avoid dried)

WHOLE SPICES
Cinnamon sticks
Black mustard seeds
Green and black cardamom pods
Black peppercorns
Cumin seeds
Coriander seeds
Fenugreek seeds
Fennel seeds
Blade mace
Cloves

GROUND SPICES, DRIED HERBS AND CANNED
AND BOTTLED INGREDIENTS
Kashmiri chilli powder
Paprika
Ground cumin
Ground coriander
Ground turmeric
Dried fenugreek leaves (kasoori methi)
Ground almonds
Coconut flour or coconut milk powder
Rapeseed (canola) oil
Mustard oil
Coconut oil
Tinned (canned) chopped tomatoes
Concentrated tomato paste

STARTERS AND SNACKS

In this chapter you will find some hugely popular starters and snacks that are ideal for entertaining outside. Whether you want to cook up a feast for your family while camping or invite all your neighbours for a barbecue to remember, you will find the starters and snacks that are sure to get the meal off to a good start.

So many 'must-try' Indian street foods are fried over fire outside. Frying food on the barbecue might seem a bit strange to some but I think the great outdoors is actually the best place to do it. This was brought home to me one afternoon when my friend Christian Stevenson, aka DJ BBQ, and I fried up some onion bhajis from my book The Curry Guy on his Weber – it's now my preferred way to deep-fry foods. No lingering smells of fried food and it is so much easier to get rid of any used oil and clean up.

HOMEMADE PAPADS
MAKES 10

Fresh papads are the best! When you purchase papads for making papadums they come dried and brittle so that they can easily be snapped in two. Since watching fresh papads being made in Kerala and then trying the difference, there was no going back! These fresh papads are dried briefly but you can still bend them without breaking. They can be roasted over a hot fire as explained below or fried. This recipe can easily be scaled up and the papads will keep for weeks in an airtight container. (Photographed on pages 19, 85, 110 and 163.)

PREP TIME: 20 MINS, PLUS DRYING TIME
COOKING TIME: 10 MINS

140g (1 cup) urad dhal flour, plus extra as needed
1 tsp salt
1 tsp bicarbonate of soda (baking soda) or papad khar
Rapeseed (canola) oil, for frying or brushing

Pour the flour into a large bowl and stir in the salt and bicarbonate of soda (baking soda). Slowly add 70ml (¼ cup) water (you may not need it all) until a soft dough forms. The dough should be slightly wet and a little difficult to work with. Place the dough on a clean surface and pound it with a pestle or rolling pin for about 10 minutes, flipping the dough from time to time. This is the classic way of making the dough; the vigorous pounding is necessary for the best results, otherwise the dough won't come together.

After about 10 minutes of pounding, you are ready to knead the dough. Squish and squeeze it in your hands for a couple of minutes. If the dough is still quite wet, add a little more flour until you have a very soft ball of dough. Divide the dough into ten smaller balls.

If you have a tortilla press, this can be used to flatten the papads. Otherwise, roll the dough balls out with a rolling pin on a lightly greased surface until paper thin. Use a knife to help remove the papads from the surface.

Transfer the flattened papads to baking trays lined with baking parchment and leave to dry in the sun for a few hours, flipping from time to time (you can also leave them somewhere warm and dry overnight). Once dried, they will be quite brittle. (In winter I place the papads next to a wood fire to dry. I have also dried them in a dehydrator and next to an electric heater.)

Now you can decide how to cook the papads. Papadams are usually deep-fried. Heat enough oil for deep-frying in a large saucepan over a high heat. When the oil reaches 180°C (355°F), carefully drop in a papad. It should puff up and become crispy in places within a few seconds of hitting the oil. Remove and drain on paper towels.

In North India, papads are often grilled. To do this, simply brush each papad with a little oil and place directly on the grill, turning with tongs every few seconds until crispy and cooked through.

NOTE
You can make flavoured papads by adding chilli flakes, finely chopped green chillies, black pepper, cumin seeds or other spices to the dough.

(GF)

GOAN CAFREAL CHICKEN WINGS
SERVES 6

In *The Curry Guy Light* I featured a cafreal masala, which was used to make a chicken cafreal curry. This is a simplified version: instead of using the masala in the famous South Indian curry, it's used as a marinade for chicken wings. You could use the same cafreal marinade with other cuts of chicken too. For that matter, it's delicious as a marinade for most meats, seafood, paneer and vegetables. Many people like to cut the tips off the chicken wings for presentation. I leave them on because I like the crispy bits.

PREP TIME: 30 MINS
COOKING TIME: 20 MINS

900g (2lb) chicken wings, skin on or off

FOR THE MARINADE
60g (2¼oz) coriander (cilantro), roughly chopped
12 green bird's eye chillies
1 generous tsp ground cumin
1 generous tsp ground coriander
½ tsp ground black pepper
½ tsp ground cinnamon
8 garlic cloves, roughly chopped
2.5cm (1in) piece of ginger, roughly chopped
½ tsp ground turmeric
1 tsp tamarind paste
2 tbsp coconut oil (optional)
Approx. 70ml (¼ cup) white wine vinegar or coconut vinegar, for blending

Put all the marinade ingredients apart from the vinegar into a blender. Blend, adding just enough vinegar to form a paste. Pour half of the paste over the wings and mix well to coat (keep the remaining marinade for later). Cover the chicken and put into the fridge, along with the reserved marinade, until ready to cook (you can do this the day before you want to cook).

When ready to cook, set up your barbecue for indirect heat cooking (see page 9). If your barbecue has an inbuilt thermometer, you're aiming for a cooking temperature of 180°C (355°F). Place a drip pan with a little water in it opposite the hot coals and arrange the chicken wings on a lightly greased cooking grill over the pan. (If using a ceramic barbecue, you do not need to use the drip pan with water.) Cover and cook for 25 minutes, or until the chicken has reached an internal temperature of 75°C (165°F). For the last 5 minutes or so of cooking, baste the chicken with the leftover marinade. Remember, you're roasting on a barbecue here, so cooking times may vary. Cook to temperature, not time.

These wings are amazing served as they are, but if you like a bit of char like I do, move them over to the hot side of the grill before serving and cook until charred and crispy.

FOR THE RED WINGS
The red wings in the photograph are easily made too. Just sprinkle with 2 tablespoons of my all-purpose rub (see page 169) and then slather with 250ml (1 cup) of my Indian-inspired all-purpose BBQ sauce (see page 166). The marinating and roasting instructions are the same as for the green cafreal wings.

MANCHURIAN CHICKEN BITES
SERVES 4 AS A STARTER

Chinese food is very popular all over India; however, these dishes are often given an Indian touch. Use two pans to make this Indo-Chinese classic and the whole dish can be cooked and served in minutes. If your grill is not large enough to hold two pans, no worries. Just cook the chicken first and then make the sauce before stirring it all up to serve. This dish can be served on its own, or with rice as a main course.

PREP TIME: 15 MINS
COOKING TIME: 25 MINS

500g (1lb 2oz) skinless chicken thighs, cut into bite-size pieces
1 medium onion, finely chopped
2 tbsp garlic and ginger paste (see page 169)
2 green bird's eye chillies, thinly sliced
20 fresh or frozen curry leaves (optional)

FOR THE MARINADE
1 tbsp Chinese rice wine or dry sherry
1 tbsp garlic and ginger paste (see page 169)
1 tbsp honey
2 tbsp light soy sauce*
1 tsp Kashmiri chilli powder
1½ tbsp cornflour (cornstarch)
1½ tbsp rapeseed (canola) oil, plus extra for shallow-frying

FOR THE SAUCE
2 tbsp light soy sauce
2 tbsp sriracha or another chilli sauce
4 tbsp ketchup
1 tbsp rice wine vinegar (or white wine or cider vinegar)
250ml (1 cup) chicken stock or water
1 tsp sugar or jaggery
2 tbsp cornflour (cornstarch), diluted with 3 tbsp water

In a large bowl, whisk together all of the marinade ingredients and add the chicken pieces. Ensure the chicken is well coated with the marinade, then cover and refrigerate until ready to cook. As with all marinated meats, the chicken will benefit from marinating overnight, but that isn't essential here.

To make the sauce, whisk together the soy sauce, sriracha, ketchup, vinegar, chicken stock or water and sugar in a small bowl. Taste and adjust by adding more soy sauce, vinegar or sugar to your own preference. Cover and refrigerate until ready to cook.

Half-fill a wok or large saucepan with oil and heat to 180°C (355°F). If you don't have a digital thermometer, test the temperature by dropping a cube of bread into the oil; if it sizzles and turns golden in 10 seconds, it's hot enough. Fry the chicken in batches until nice and crispy – this should take a couple of minutes for each batch. Drain on paper towels, then set aside while you prepare the sauce.

Heat 2 tablespoons of the oil you used to fry the chicken in another saucepan over a medium heat. When hot, add the chopped onion and fry for about 3 minutes, or until soft. Stir in the garlic and ginger paste and chillies and fry for a further 30 seconds. Add the curry leaves, if using, and fry again for 30 seconds.

Pour in the prepared sauce and simmer for about 5 minutes until reduced and syrupy. Add the diluted cornflour mixture gradually until the sauce is thickened to your preferred consistency and then stir in the fried chicken. Continue simmering until the sauce has thickened and is sticking to the chicken pieces.

ALTERNATIVE COOKING METHOD
Although not as common, you could also skewer the chicken and grill it over hot coals until charred in places and cooked through. If doing this, leave the cornflour (cornstarch) out of the marinade.

NOTE
*Some brands of soy sauce contain gluten. Use a gluten-free version if you need this dish to be gluten-free.

TANDOORI CHICKEN LEGS TWO WAYS
SERVES 3–4

This is a recipe I make often for my family. We all have our own spice preferences – I make the mild version for my daughters and the spicier version for the rest of us. It's a fun way to prepare chicken; the bare bones work as handles for the delicious meat, but if you're short on time you can skip that step or use another cut of meat. If you can't get hold of chicken leg portions, you can use ready-jointed thighs and drumsticks; just be aware that these are often smaller in size so you may want to up the quantity.

PREP TIME: 20 MINS, PLUS
MARINATING TIME
COOKING TIME: 15–20 MINS

8 whole chicken legs, skinned and separated into thighs and drumsticks
5 garlic cloves, finely chopped
2 tbsp lemon juice
½ tsp salt
30 raw unsalted cashew nuts
15g (1 cup) coriander (cilantro), roughly chopped
5cm (2in) piece of ginger, peeled and roughly chopped
2 green bird's eye chillies, roughly chopped
1 blade mace (about 2.5cm/1in)
Seeds from 4 green cardamom pods
125g (½ cup) Greek yoghurt, whisked
4 generous tbsp ghee
1½ tbsp Kashmiri chilli powder
1 tbsp paprika
½ tsp ground turmeric
Lemon wedges, to serve
Chaat masala, to serve (optional; see page 168)

To make each chicken handle, use a sharp knife to cut around and along the bone, starting at the thinner end, and carefully move the meat towards the other end. You should be left with nice balls of meat and a bone handle for picking up and eating. Remove any stringy white tendons from the drumstick bone with a sharp knife or scissors.

Put the prepared chicken into a large bowl and rub with the garlic, lemon juice and salt. Cover and set aside while you make the marinade: put the cashew nuts into a blender with just enough water to blend to a smooth paste. Add the coriander (cilantro), ginger, chillies, mace and cardamom seeds and blend again. Whisk this paste into the yoghurt.

Take half of the prepared chicken pieces, place them in another bowl and pour over half of the marinade. This is the milder version. Cover and put in the fridge to marinate for at least 1 hour.

Next, melt the ghee in a small frying pan and then stir in the chilli powder, paprika and turmeric. Allow to cool slightly and then pour this mixture into the remaining marinade and whisk until smooth. Pour over the remaining chicken pieces and rub it into the flesh. Cover and put in the fridge to marinate for 1 hour, or overnight.

When ready to cook, prepare a multi-level direct heat fire (see page 10). When the coals are white-hot and it is uncomfortable to hold your hand 5cm (2in) above the grill for more than 2 seconds, it's ready. Weave skewers through the chicken pieces so that they are secure. Rub as much marinade off the meat as possible and retain. Place the skewered chicken legs over the fire and cook for 5 minutes without turning, then flip over to cook the other side. Rotate from time to time so that the chicken cooks evenly, basting with the leftover marinades.

When the chicken is nicely charred and cooked through, remove from the heat to rest for a few minutes before removing the meat from the skewers. If you have a meat thermometer, check that the chicken has an internal temperature of 75°C (165°F), although the meat will continue to cook while resting on the hot skewers. Serve with lemon wedges. A little chaat masala sprinkled over the top is a nice touch.

CHICKEN BREASTS STUFFED WITH CHEESE AND SPINACH

SERVES 4–6

I like to cook these chicken breasts over indirect heat, which gives them a lightly smoked flavour. You could also cook them in a pan or directly on the grill over direct heat. The sliced stuffed chicken breasts are a great way to start off a meal, or they could also be served as a main. I like to marinate the chicken in tandoori marinade first (see page 53), but it's still delicious without.

PREP TIME: 15 MINS, PLUS MARINATING TIME (OPTIONAL)
COOKING TIME: 20 MINS

4 large skinless chicken breasts
1 batch tandoori marinade (see page 53), mixed with 2 tbsp Greek yoghurt (optional)
2 tbsp ghee, plus extra for greasing
½ onion, finely chopped
2 tbsp garlic and ginger paste (see page 169)
1 tsp garam masala (see page 168)
2 green chillies, finely chopped (more or less to taste)
400g (14oz) baby spinach leaves, washed and squeezed dry
300g (10½oz) paneer cheese, grated
Salt and freshly ground black pepper, to taste

Using a very sharp knife, slice the chicken breasts lengthways through the centre, but not completely through, to butterfly. Open out the chicken breasts and lay them flat on a clean surface. Cover with cling film (plastic wrap) and flatten with a mallet or other heavy object such as a rolling pin. If marinating, place the flattened chicken breasts in a dish with the marinade, cover and leave to marinate in the fridge for up to 48 hours.

Heat the ghee in a large frying pan over a medium heat and add the chopped onion. Fry for about 5 minutes, or until soft and translucent. Add the garlic and ginger paste, the garam masala, the chopped chillies and the spinach and cook over a high heat until the spinach is just slightly wilted. Season the spinach mixture with a little salt and pepper, remove from the pan, squeeze dry and chop finely.

Now divide the spinach filling between the four flattened chicken breasts and top with the grated paneer. Roll up the breasts lengthways and secure by tying with string (twine).

When ready to cook, set up your barbecue for indirect heat cooking (see page 9). You are aiming for a steady cooking temperature of 200°C (400°F). Place the rolled chicken breasts on a lightly greased cooking grate and cook for about 15 minutes, or until cooked through and lightly browned. Be sure to cook to temperature and not time. The chicken is ready when it reaches an internal temperature of 75°C (165°F).

Transfer the chicken to a cutting board and slice diagonally into 2.5cm (1in) thick pieces. Sprinkle with a little more salt and freshly ground black pepper before serving.

TANDOORI MUTTON BURRA KEBABS

SERVES 8

Although these chops make an outstanding main course dish, I usually serve them as a starter, followed by a good curry like the chicken sali (see page 97) or chicken ghee roast (see page 100). The idea behind this is to use that beautiful fire you've built in more than one way, while bringing two completely different courses to the table. These chops are the perfect start to any meal, washed down with a few cold beers. You can always halve the recipe if serving fewer people. Burra kebabs are traditionally made with mutton chops but you could use lamb with equally delicious results.

PREP TIME: 10 MINS, PLUS MARINATING TIME
COOKING TIME: 10 MINS

16 mutton or lamb chops (about 1kg/2lb 4oz)
Melted ghee, for basting

FOR THE FIRST MARINADE

½ red onion, blended to a paste with a little water
2 tbsp garlic and ginger paste (see page 169)
1½ tbsp Kashmiri chilli powder (more or less to taste)
½ tsp salt, plus extra to taste

FOR THE SECOND MARINADE

2 generous tbsp Greek yoghurt, whisked
1 tbsp rapeseed (canola) oil or mustard oil
1 tbsp distilled white vinegar
1 tbsp garlic and ginger paste (see page 169)
1 tsp dried fenugreek leaves (kasoori methi)
1 tbsp garam masala (see page 168)

TO SERVE

1 onion, thinly sliced
Lime wedges
Green chutney (see page 162)

Put the lamb or mutton chops into a large bowl, add all of the ingredients for the first marinade and rub into the meat. Really get it into the flesh. Set aside while you prepare the second marinade. Put the ingredients for the second marinade into a bowl and whisk until smooth. Now rub this marinade into the chops and leave to marinate, covered, in the fridge for at least 2 hours, or up to 48 hours. The longer the better.

Remove the marinated chops from the fridge at least 30 minutes before cooking. Prepare a direct heat multi-level fire (see page 10), so that you have an intense heat but also a cooler place to move the chops once they have finished cooking. Skewer the chops by weaving the skewers through the meat twice, so that they are secure.

Place the skewered chops over the hot fire and cook for 5 minutes, or until the underside is beginning to sizzle and char. Then flip them over to cook the other side. These chops can move on the skewer, making it difficult to cook both sides, so feel free to use your hands and prop them up against each other to ensure a good, even cook.

As the meat cooks, drizzle with a little ghee from time to time. The ghee will drop into the coals and cause a large flame, but it will soon die down, so don't worry. The chops are ready when cooked through and nicely charred all over. Serve with the sliced onions, lime wedges and a good chutney, like coriander and mint.

NOTE

Burra kebabs are traditionally cooked over hot fire on skewers. You could cheat, though, and cook them over direct heat on a lightly greased cooking grate. This will make char line marks, so the kebabs will look different, but they will be just as delicious.

CHICKEN AND LAMB KEBABS
SERVES 4

This is a really fun seekh kebab recipe that is as delicious as it is impressive. First you cook lamb kebabs and let them cool on the skewer, then you cover those kebabs with the chicken kebab mixture. Cooking seekh kebabs on skewers takes some practice. It is far easier to just form the sausage-shaped seekh kebabs without a skewer and cook them on the grill, but I promise you, once you master the art of making them on skewers, there's no going back. I usually make normal lamb seekh kebabs and chicken seekh kebabs with half the full recipe for each and then use the remaining meat from each batch to make these special kebabs. For best results, be sure to read my instructions on preparing seekh kebabs on page 39.

PREP TIME: 30 MINS
COOKING TIME: 25 MINS

oil, for greasing
½ batch chilled lamb seekh
   kebab mixture (see page 45)
½ batch chilled chicken seekh
   kebab mixture (see page 43)
3 tbsp melted ghee, for basting
Hot sauce or raita, to serve

Lightly grease a skewer with oil and wet your hands, then take a pool-ball-sized ball of the chilled lamb mixture and slide it onto the skewer. Now start squeezing the ball into a long sausage shape. It is important that you squeeze really tightly to get the meat to adhere to the skewer. It is also important that you get the kebab as uniform as possible. It should look like a long sausage that is the same thickness all the way down the skewer with no bits hanging off. Once you think the meat is securely on the skewer, shake it a few times. If it stays on, it should be OK, but if it falls off at the shaking stage, you need to squeeze it on tighter. Repeat with the remaining lamb mixture; I make 4 large skewers but you could make more if you use smaller skewers.

Prepare a multi-level direct heat fire (see page 10). When the coals are white-hot and it is uncomfortable to hold your hand 5cm (2in) above the grill for more than 2 seconds, you're ready to cook. Place the skewers over the hot coals and cook on one side until browned, about 5 minutes, then rotate the skewers to cook the other side. Rotate often so the kebabs cook evenly.

Once cooked through, transfer the skewers to a plate to cool. They will need to be at least room temperature before proceeding with the next part of the recipe. You can also make these ahead, chill them once cool and then use them cold from the fridge. When the meat has cooled, carefully squeeze balls of the cold chicken kebab mixture around the lamb skewers, squeezing tightly with wet hands until you can shake it without the meat falling off.

Place the finished skewers over the fire to cook for 5 minutes, then rotate to cook the other side and start basting with ghee. Continue basting and rotating until the chicken is cooked through. If you have a meat thermometer, check that the chicken is cooked to 75°C (165°F). Serve immediately with hot sauce or a good raita.

KASHMIRI KABARGAH MUTTON CHOPS
SERVES 4

In India, mutton often refers to goat meat and this recipe is really good when made with goat, too. I have described the Kashmiri way of making these amazing chops, marinating them and then frying. If you would rather place your chops on the grill instead of frying them, go for it. That's nice too. Just grill over direct heat until charred and cooked to your liking.

PREP TIME: 15 MINS
COOKING TIME: 40 MINS

3 tbsp gram (chickpea) flour
8 double-cut bone-in lamb or mutton chops
500ml (2 cups) full-fat (whole) milk, plus extra as needed
½ tsp cloves
1 tsp fennel seeds
1 blade mace (about 2.5cm/1in)
5cm (2in) cinnamon stick
3 green cardamom pods, lightly bruised
1 onion, quartered
2 tbsp garlic and ginger paste (see page 169)
Juice of 1 lemon
2 tbsp Greek yoghurt, whisked
1 tbsp Kashmiri chilli powder
1 tsp ground cumin
1 tsp ground coriander
1 tsp salt, or to taste
Rapeseed (canola) oil, for frying
Lemon wedges, to serve
Flaky sea salt, to serve

Place a frying pan over a medium heat and toast the gram (chickpea) flour for a couple of minutes, stirring continuously until fragrant and about two tones darker in colour. Set aside.

Place the lamb or mutton chops in a saucepan and pour the milk over them. The meat should be completely covered with liquid, so add more milk if needed. Stir in the cloves, fennel seeds, mace, cinnamon stick, cardamom pods and onion and bring to a simmer. Cook for 30 minutes and then remove the meat from the milk and pat dry.

Place the chops in a large bowl and coat with the garlic and ginger paste, lemon juice, yoghurt, chilli powder, cumin, coriander and salt. Once thoroughly coated, add the toasted gram flour and mix well with your hands. You can start cooking immediately or let the meat marinate in the fridge for up to 48 hours.

When ready to cook, heat about 2.5cm (1in) rapeseed (canola) oil in a frying pan over a high heat. When visibly hot, add the chops and fry for about 3 minutes until charred, then flip over to cook the other side. Continue cooking until charred and crispy in places. Drain on paper towels before serving with lemon wedges and flaky sea salt.

NOTE

Although the traditional way to finish these chops is to fry them, they are also amazing grilled over a high heat on a cooking grate or skewered and cooked until charred to your liking. You can, however, get a delicious smoky flavour to the fried chops by using the dhungar method, which involves using a piece of burning charcoal to smoke the marinated meat. I find it easiest to do this by marinating the meat in a lidded wok. Make a well in the centre of the meat, then fold a sheet of foil in half and place a piece of burning charcoal on top. Put this into the well in the centre of the meat and drizzle with 1 tablespoon of ghee – it will begin to smoke. Immediately cover the wok and leave until almost all of the smoke has subsided. Cook as above.

RECHEADO FISH PLATTER
SERVES 4

The paste used in this recipe is ideal for stuffing fish, meat and vegetables but it can also be used as a marinade. Recheado masala is a Portuguese-inspired recipe from Goa, recheado meaning 'stuffed'. It is much more common to fry recheado fish but I like to char it over the fire. If you would like to fry it, just cover the bottom of a frying pan with oil and fry over direct heat until cooked through and crispy on both sides.

PREP TIME: 15 MINS, PLUS SOAKING TIME
COOKING TIME: 10 MINS

1kg (2lb 4oz) fish such as sardines or mackerel, fins snipped off
Flaky sea salt, to serve
Lemon wedges, to serve

FOR THE RECHEADO PASTE
25 dried Kashmiri chillies, roughly chopped (remove the seeds if you don't want it super-hot)
1 tsp black peppercorns
1 tsp cumin seeds
6 cloves
6 fenugreek seeds
1 tsp mustard seeds
2 tbsp rapeseed (canola) oil
2 red onions, finely chopped
3 red bird's eye chillies
5cm (2in) piece of ginger, peeled and roughly chopped
10 garlic cloves, smashed and roughly chopped
$\frac{1}{2}$ tsp ground cinnamon
$\frac{1}{2}$ tsp ground turmeric
1 tbsp paprika
1 tsp sugar
1 tsp tamarind paste (the 'paste' I use is labelled 'concentrate')
70ml ($\frac{1}{4}$ cup) palm vinegar (or white wine or cider vinegar)
Salt, to taste

Place the fish on a board and scrape as much moisture out of the skin as you can using a sharp knife, then score the fish a few times on each side. Cover and place in the fridge while you prepare the marinade.

Heat a frying pan over a medium-high heat and toast the chillies for about 2 minutes until fragrant. Be sure to move them around in the pan so that they toast evenly, then tip into a bowl and cover with water. Let stand for 20 minutes. Meanwhile, toast the whole spices in the same pan over a medium heat until fragrant but not yet smoking and then transfer to a plate to cool.

Next, pour the oil into the pan and fry the onions over a medium heat for about 7 minutes until soft, transparent and lightly caramelized. Pour the fried onions, drained chillies, toasted whole spices and the remaining ingredients apart from the salt into a spice grinder or blender and blend to a smooth paste. The recheado paste should be quite red. If you want it to be more red, you could add more paprika or even some more toasted chillies. Taste and add salt if you wish. You could also add a little more sugar if you want it sweeter.

Rub the paste all over and inside the fish, ensuring that you get the marinade right into the slits you made. Set to one side to marinate while you fire up the grill.

Many people use fish baskets to grill fish on the barbecue and if you have one, you could definitely use it here as I did in the photograph opposite; however, you could also cook the fish without a basket. Prepare a hot, direct heat fire, lightly brush the cooking grate with oil and when it is uncomfortable to hold your hand 5cm (2in) above the grill for more than 2 seconds, place your fish on it. Grill on one side until the fish comes away from the grill naturally and without sticking. A good metal spatula will help with this but don't force it. The fish will come away once the skin has charred a bit. Flip and cook the other side until equally charred. Check; if by chance the fish isn't completely cooked through, just continue cooking for a couple more minutes. Depending on how charred the skin is, you might want to continue cooking over a cooler part of the fire.

Sprinkle with a little flaky sea salt and serve with lemon wedges.

CHARGRILLED STUFFED CHILLIES
SERVES 4–6

Stuffed, grilled and fried chillies and (bell) peppers are very popular all over India. In my book *The Curry Guy Veggie*, I featured a fried, stuffed chilli recipe, so I thought it would be a good move to show you this, my favourite way to cook chillies – stuffed and chargrilled! This recipe makes a delicious light lunch or side dish. Although I like preparing and cooking this whole recipe on the barbecue, you could of course prepare the stuffing indoors and stuff the chillies before taking them out to the grill to cook.

PREP TIME: 25 MINS
COOKING TIME: 1½ HOURS

2 tbsp salt, plus extra to taste
500g (1lb 2oz) long green chillies, sliced lengthways and deseeded
2 tbsp garlic and ginger paste (see page 169)
1 tsp lemon juice
Rapeseed (canola) oil, for greasing
1 potato
1 large onion, unpeeled
3 tbsp melted ghee
1 tsp mustard seeds
½ tsp cumin seeds
10 curry leaves, roughly chopped
1 large tomato, diced
½ tsp asafoetida
½ tsp ground turmeric
½ tsp Kashmiri chilli powder
½ tsp amchoor (dried mango powder)
100g (3½oz) paneer cheese, grated
3 tbsp chopped coriander (cilantro)
Lime quarters, for squeezing

Prepare a direct heat fire large enough to burn for about 90 minutes. When the coals are white-hot and it is uncomfortable to hold your hand 5cm (2in) above the grill for more than 2 seconds, you're ready to cook.

Bring a large saucepan of water to a boil, stir in the salt and add the chillies. Remove from the heat and cover. Allow the chillies to sit in the water for 15 minutes, then drain and transfer to a bowl to cool slightly. Stir in the garlic and ginger paste and lemon juice and set aside.

Lightly oil the potato and double wrap it with foil. Place the wrapped potato and the whole onion right down in the burning embers and leave to cook for 40–60 minutes, moving them around from time to time so that they cook evenly.

Once the onion and potato are soft and cooked through, remove from the embers. Scoop out the potato flesh from the skin and finely chop the smoky onion. Heat a frying pan over a high heat and add two tablespoons of the ghee. When visibly hot, stir in the mustard seeds and when they begin to crackle, add the cumin seeds and chopped curry leaves. Allow to sizzle for about 30 seconds and then add the chopped onion, diced tomato and the ground spices. Stir well and then fold in the paneer, cooked potato and coriander (cilantro). Season with salt to taste.

Allow the stuffing mixture to cool slightly and then use it to fill each of the chillies. Lightly brush the cooking grate with a little oil and place the stuffed chillies over the fire. Cook on one side until grill marks appear. Baste with a little of the remaining melted ghee and turn over to cook the other side. Baste again with the ghee. The chillies are ready when nicely charred and heated through. Serve with lime quarters for squeezing.

NOTE
To reduce the time it takes to make this recipe, finely chop the raw onion and potato and fry with the other stuffing ingredients until cooked through; the dish won't be as smoky but will still be very good.

EASY SPICY GRILLED PRAWNS
SERVES 4–6 AS A STARTER

This is a good one to start any outdoor meal. The preparation is super simple and the prawns (shrimp) grill to perfection in minutes. Get these delicious grilled prawns on the table to curb your guests' hunger and you can relax while you cook the rest of the meal. You could also cook them with a selection of kebabs and serve as your main course. The recheado paste on page 26 is also really good on grilled prawns.

PREP TIME: 10 MINS
COOKING TIME: 10 MINS

500g (1lb 2oz) medium-sized raw prawns (shrimp), peeled and deveined
½ tsp ground turmeric
1 tbsp Kashmiri chilli powder
1 tbsp garam masala (see page 168)
70ml (¼ cup) melted ghee
1½ tbsp garlic and ginger paste (see page 169)
Salt, to taste
Lime wedges, to serve

Put the prawns (shrimp) into a bowl, add the spices, 2 tablespoons of the melted ghee and the garlic and ginger paste and rub all over the prawns. Set aside to marinate while you start up your fire. Prepare a multi-level direct heat fire (see page 10) and when it's uncomfortable to hold your hand 5cm (2in) above where your skewers will sit for more than 2 seconds, you're ready to cook.

Skewer the prawns and place them over the fire. Rotate from time to time so that they char evenly and cook through. As you cook, baste the prawns with the remaining melted ghee. This might cause a small flare up, but it rarely lasts long and you can move the prawns off the heat if needed.

Season with salt and serve hot, right off the skewers, with lime wedges to squeeze over.

SPICY STUFFED MUSSELS
SERVES 6

I first tried these fried mussels at a toddy shack near Munnar, Kerala. As I was enjoying the toddy so much the owners were happy to let me watch them prepare this signature dish. The stuffed mussels were cooked in hot oil over a coconut shell fire, which added to the whole experience. They could just be the perfect starter course. Unfortunately, we can't get homemade toddy here in the UK, but these mussels are also amazing necked back with a few cold beers.

PREP TIME: 25 MINS
COOKING TIME: 10 MINS

1 coconut, shelled and flesh shredded (or use approx. 400g/14oz frozen shredded coconut)
1 large red onion, roughly chopped
10 green bird's eye chillies, roughly chopped (more or less to taste)
10 garlic cloves, roughly chopped
30g (1 packed cup) coriander (cilantro), roughly chopped
2 tbsp fennel seeds
½ tsp ground turmeric
1 tsp salt
400g (2½ cups) rice flour
60g (½ cup) plain (all purpose) flour
1kg (2lb 4oz) large live mussels
Rapeseed (canola) oil, for frying
Lemon wedges, to serve
Sauces and chutneys of your choice (see pages 161–167), to serve (optional)

FOR THE OPTIONAL SPICE COATING
½ tsp ground turmeric
½ tsp salt
2 tbsp Kashmiri chilli powder
Juice of 1 lime

To make the optional spice coating, mix together all the ingredients in a bowl with just enough fresh water to make a thick paste. Set aside.

Put the shredded coconut, onion, green chillies, garlic, coriander (cilantro), fennel seeds, turmeric and salt into blender and blend to a fine paste, adding a drop of water if needed. Transfer this mixture to a bowl, add the flours and bring together, adding a little water at a time, until you have a soft, workable dough. If you happen to add too much water, just add some more rice flour. Knead for a couple of minutes and then cover and put in the fridge until ready to use.

Clean and debeard the mussels under a cold running tap and discard any that don't close tightly when tapped or that have broken shells. Prepare a hot direct heat fire (see page 10) in a kettle or ceramic barbecue. If you don't have a barbecue with a lid, find something to cover the mussels with while they are cooking, like a metal bowl.

When the coals are white-hot and it is uncomfortable to hold your hand 5cm (2in) above the grill for more than 2 seconds, you're ready to cook. Tip the cleaned mussels right onto the grill and close the lid. After about 3 minutes, open the lid. If the mussels haven't all opened, stir them around a bit on the grate and close the lid again for another couple of minutes. Once cooked, transfer the mussels to a clean work surface and discard any that didn't open.

Now half-fill a wok or high-sided frying pan with rapeseed (canola) oil and bring up to 180°C (355°F) on the grate over the hottest part of the grill. It is important not to get the oil too hot, so ensure you have a cool side of the grill to place the pan on if needed. While the oil is heating up, open the mussel shells, leaving the hinge connected, and loosen the mussel away from the shell. Take a small ball of the dough mixture and use it to fill the shell, securing the mussel in place. If using the spice coating, roll the stuffed mussels in the paste to coat. Fry in batches for about 3 minutes, or until golden brown. Keep warm while you are cooking the remaining mussels.

These mussels are great on their own, but you could also serve them with lemon wedges and your favourite raita, green chutney, chilli sauce or chilli oil.

Clockwise from top left: Easy spicy grilled prawns (page 29); chargrilled stuffed chillies (page 28); spicy stuffed mussels

VEGETABLE SKEWERS
SERVES 4

Go for colourful, seasonal vegetables here and you really can't go wrong. If using harder vegetables such as potato, be sure to par-cook first and then finish cooking over the fire.

PREP TIME: 10 MINS, PLUS MARINATING TIME
COOKING TIME: 10–15 MINS

About 600g (1lb 5oz) mixed vegetables, such as (bell) peppers, tomatoes, mushrooms, onions, potatoes, courgettes (zucchini)
Flaky sea salt, to taste
Green chutney (see page 162), to serve

FOR THE MARINADE
1 tsp ground cumin
1 tsp ground coriander
1 tsp garam masala (see page 168)
1 tsp Kashmiri chilli powder
1 tsp chaat masala (see page 168)
½ tsp ground turmeric
1 tsp ground black pepper
2 tsp gram (chickpea) flour
2 tbsp garlic and ginger paste (see page 169)
½ tsp dried fenugreek leaves (kasoori methi)
2 tsp rapeseed (canola) oil
250g (1 cup) Greek yoghurt, whisked

First whisk together all of the marinade ingredients in a large bowl.

Next prepare your vegetables. You want the pieces to be about the same size. Add the cut vegetables to the marinade, stir and allow to marinate for 30 minutes to 1 hour.

Prepare a direct heat fire (see page 10). When the coals are white-hot and it is uncomfortable to hold your hand 5cm (2in) above the grill for more than 2 seconds, you're ready to cook.

Thread the vegetables onto skewers, then place the skewers over the hot coals. You can also set the skewers on a cooking grate if preferred. Cook for 5–10 minutes until cooked through and charred in places. Season with flaky sea salt to taste and serve with green chutney.

TANDOORI ARTICHOKES
SERVES 2–4

I came up with this recipe while visiting my parents back in California. I used fresh artichokes, which I boiled until the hearts were tender, but in the UK I usually use tinned (canned) brined artichokes or the frozen artichoke hearts available at Asian grocers. This marinade is also great teamed with cauliflower and other veggies, by the way.

PREP TIME: 10 MINS
COOKING TIME: 10 MINS

400g (14oz) cooked artichoke hearts

FOR THE MARINADE
1 tbsp rapeseed (canola) oil
2 tbsp Greek yoghurt, whisked
Juice of 1 lemon
1½ tbsp garlic and ginger paste (see page 169)
1 tsp ground cumin
½ tsp ground coriander
1 tsp Kashmiri chilli powder
½ tsp ground turmeric
½ tsp garam masala (see page 168)
½ tsp amchoor (dried mango powder)
Salt, to taste
Kebab-shop garlic sauce (see page 165), to serve (optional)

Whisk together all of the marinade ingredients in a bowl and stir in the artichoke hearts. Leave to marinate while you start your fire.

Prepare a direct heat fire (see page 10) and skewer the artichoke hearts. When the coals are white-hot and it is uncomfortable to hold your hand 5cm (2in) above the grill for more than 2 seconds, you're ready to cook.

Thread the artichokes onto skewers, then place the skewers over the fire and cook, rotating from time to time, until heated through and nicely charred. This should take 6–10 minutes.

Serve hot, just as they are, or with kebab-shop garlic sauce.

PANEER POPCORN

SERVES 6

I first tried these at a beach bar in Goa and they reminded me of fried mozzarella sticks, though they are a little less gooey. Obviously influenced by Italian cuisine, paneer popcorn is still distinctively Indian in flavour and texture and I think it makes the perfect outdoor party snack. Try them with a good dipping sauce such as the kebab-shop red chilli sauce on page 165.

PREP TIME: 10 MINS
COOKING TIME: 10 MINS

400g (14oz) paneer cheese, cut into bite-size cubes
1 tbsp rapeseed (canola) oil, plus extra for frying
1 tsp salt
2 tsp Kashmiri chilli powder
1 tsp garlic granules
1 tsp dried mixed Italian herbs
1 tsp ground black pepper
3 eggs
120g (1 cup) fine breadcrumbs, homemade or shop-bought
Kebab-shop red chilli sauce (see page 165), to serve

Put the cubed paneer into a bowl with the oil, salt, chilli powder, garlic granules, Italian herbs and black pepper. Mix well with your hands to combine. Beat the eggs in a bowl and pour the breadcrumbs into another bowl.

Dip the paneer cubes into the beaten egg and then coat with the breadcrumbs. Once all the cubes have been coated with the egg and breadcrumbs, dip them back into the egg and coat again with the breadcrumbs.

Heat 10cm (4in) oil in a large saucepan or karahi over a high heat. When the oil reaches 180°C (355°F), you're ready to get cooking. Fry the paneer in batches until crispy and browned. This should take about 3 minutes per batch. Transfer to paper towels to soak up any excess oil and serve hot with kebab-shop chilli sauce.

MASALA POPPED SORGHUM

SERVES 4

Beer and popcorn around a roaring fire: who wouldn't love that? Sorghum is India's version of popcorn. Yes, they eat popcorn in India too, but popped sorghum goes back much further. Popped sorghum is quite similar in flavour to popcorn, but I prefer it – especially when mixed with the buttery spice mixture below and a squeeze or two of lime juice. We are talking addictive here! I have given a weight for the sorghum here, but it is important that it lies in one layer at the bottom of your pan.

PREP TIME: 5 MINS
COOKING TIME: 10 MINS

2 tbsp rapeseed (canola) oil
180g (1 cup) sorghum
2–3 tbsp ghee or butter
½ tsp Kashmiri chilli powder
1 tsp ground cumin
1 tsp ground coriander
1 tsp garam masala (see page 168)
½ tsp fine sea salt
2 limes cut into wedges, to serve

Heat the oil in a saucepan over a medium heat. You might need to play with this a bit when cooking over a fire, as if the pan is not hot enough, the kernels won't pop, but if it's too hot they will burn. Add the sorghum in one layer, cover the saucepan with a vented lid, just like you would when cooking popcorn, and wait for the kernels to start popping. Shake the pan from time to time to ensure nothing is burning. When the kernels stop popping, take the pan off the heat.

Melt the ghee or butter in a frying pan over a medium-high heat and then stir in the spices and salt. Stir this mixture into the popped sorghum and serve immediately with lime wedges to squeeze over the top.

TANDOORI STUFFED POTATOES
SERVES 6

If you're up for a challenge, try this recipe exactly as written. However, you can still get excellent results by following the simplified method in the Note below.

PREP TIME: 1 HOUR
COOKING TIME: 30 MINS

1kg (2lb 4oz) potatoes (about 8), peeled
1 tsp ground turmeric
1 tbsp salt
2 tbsp rapeseed (canola) oil or ghee
150g (5½oz) very finely chopped vegetables of your choice, such as carrots, onions, (bell) peppers, green bird's eye chillies, tomatoes
5 garlic cloves, finely chopped
2.5cm (1in) piece of ginger, finely chopped
1 tsp Kashmiri chilli powder
1 tsp chaat masala (see page 168)
2 tsp ground coriander
2 tsp ground cumin
10 roasted cashew nuts, roughly chopped
200g (7oz) paneer cheese, grated
50g (2oz) strong Cheddar cheese, grated
3 generous tbsp finely chopped coriander (cilantro)
1 batch tandoori marinade (see page 53, or use shop-bought)
2 tbsp melted ghee, for basting
Green chutney (see page 162), to serve
Roasted onion raita (see page) 161, to serve

Using an apple corer, hollow out the centre of the potatoes. If you are cooking this in a tandoor (see page 7), leave two of the potatoes with one end intact; these will go at the end of the vertical skewers to stop the filling sliding off into the fire. Hollow out most of them all the way through so that there is plenty of room for stuffing. Next, carefully trim the potatoes with a potato peeler until you have cylindrical tubes with straight sides. Be sure to retain half of the potato cores.

Put the prepared potatoes into a large bowl of water and swirl them around a bit to remove any excess starch. Drain and add new water and set aside. This is especially important if you aren't cooking everything immediately, so that the potatoes don't discolour.

Bring a large saucepan of water to a boil and stir in the turmeric and salt. Add the potatoes and simmer for about 7 minutes, or until the potatoes are about 80% cooked. Drain and set aside.

Next finely chop the reserved potato cores. Heat the 2 tablespoons of oil or ghee in a frying pan over a high heat. When hot, add the chopped potatoes and the other vegetables and fry until the potatoes are soft. Stir in the chopped garlic and ginger, ground spices, chopped cashew nuts, grated cheeses and chopped coriander (cilantro). Take off the heat to cool slightly.

Fill the hollowed-out potatoes with the vegetable mixture and then dip each one in the tandoori marinade. Skewer the potatoes, three on each skewer, with the two potatoes that have not been completely hollowed out at the end of the skewers if cooking in a tandoor.

Prepare a direct heat fire (see page 10). When the coals are white-hot and it is uncomfortable to hold your hand 5cm (2in) above the grill for more than 2 seconds, you're ready to cook. Grill over the hot coals for 10–15 minutes, or until nicely charred on the exterior. Baste the potatoes with a little ghee as they cook for extra flavour. Slice and serve with green chutney and/or roasted onion raita.

NOTE

For a simpler method, double wrap the whole potatoes in foil and place in the embers to cook for an hour. Then cut off the tops and scoop out the flesh. Make the stuffing, using the recipe above, and use to fill the potato skins. Place the tops back on the potatoes and secure with toothpicks, then rub the skin with oil or tandoori marinade and cook over indirect heat at 200°C (400°F) for about 10 minutes.

GRILLED TANDOORI PINEAPPLE
SERVES 4

Sweet, mildly spiced, sour and savoury, this tandoori pineapple recipe is a refreshing way to start or finish a meal on a sunny day. The best way to approach this recipe is by thinking about your own flavour preferences. If you think pineapple is sweet enough, for example, leave out the optional honey (it does add to the caramelization though). You can also adjust the amount of chilli powder used, but I think the mild Kashmiri chilli powder gives the pineapple a nice hit.

PREP TIME: 10 MINS
COOKING TIME: 10 MINS

1 large pineapple, peeled and cut into two-bite chunks
2 tbsp melted ghee or butter
Flaky sea salt, to taste

FOR THE MARINADE
1½ tsp Kashmiri chilli powder
½ tsp chaat masala (see page 168)
½ tsp ground black pepper
1 tsp honey (optional)
2 tsp lemon juice

Whisk together all of the marinade ingredients in a large bowl and add the pineapple pieces. Stir well so that the pineapple chunks are evenly coated and then transfer to skewers. Prepare a direct heat fire (see page 10), then grill the pineapple skewers until lightly charred. Baste each piece liberally with the melted ghee or butter and cook for a further 30 seconds. Serve sprinkled with a little flaky sea salt.

GRILLED, BARBECUED AND SKEWERED MAINS

As I mentioned at the beginning of this book, most of these recipes can be cooked on a simple kettle-style barbecue. The instructions for grilling, barbecuing and roasting in the individual recipes are pretty straightforward. However, cooking on skewers can be a bit daunting at first, so I have outlined some key tips opposite.

One of the most important things I hope you take away with you is that these recipes are not set in stone! Feel free to adjust them by cooking in the way you prefer. Skewered seekh kebabs could be simplified by cooking without the skewers on the grill or in a pan. Barbecued tandoori chicken could be cooked over a low, direct heat and turned often. Experiment and have fun!

A WORD ON SKEWERS

Cooking on a skewer is one of the most enjoyable and popular ways to cook over fire. Over the years I have acquired a good collection of metal skewers in varying shapes and sizes and I prefer different skewers when cooking different recipes. To get started, however, a few standard metal skewers will be fine. You will see from the photographs the benefits of using different-sized skewers for some recipes, but it's not essential.

Wooden skewers can also be used instead of metal skewers, but they do need to be soaked for at least 30 minutes before using.

At the end of the day, you just want to cook up some awesome tasting food and that can also be done directly on the cooking grate without using skewers at all. So if you don't have any skewers that will work, no worries. Just cook these recipes on the cooking grate.

SEEKH KEBABS

This brings me to the most difficult skewering to get right... the seekh kebab. Making seekh kebabs can be a bit tricky if you've never made them before. I've heard so many stories from people who have prepared their seekh kebab meat and were really looking forward to eating them, just to have the meat fall off the skewer into the fire. Don't let that happen to you! Just keep these tips in mind and you will enjoy those kebabs as they should be.

1. Always use cold minced (ground) meat right out of the fridge. I place my seekh kebab mix in the fridge for at least 2 hours before cooking.

2. If using onion, be sure to squeeze as much moisture out of it as possible before adding it to the mix. This isn't essential but squeezing out that excess moisture sure helps to keep the meat on the skewers when you're first starting out.

3. Lightly grease your skewers. This will make removing the seekh kebabs easier when cooked.

4. Use wet hands to form the seekh kebabs. Not only is it easier, but it will also give the seekh kebabs a more classic and uniform finish.

5. If cooking in a tandoor, be sure to put a piece of potato at the end of the skewer to catch the seekh kebab should it decide to try to slide off.

6. Watch the kebabs as they cook and be sure to rotate them from time to time so that they cook evenly.

7. Basting regularly with melted ghee will add to the flavour and presentation.

8. Remember: if you would rather not take your chances, you can always cook your seekh kebabs on the cooking grate. This will of course leave grill lines on your seekh kebabs, but the flavour will still be as good.

SKEWERED MEAT

Have you ever gone to rotate skewered pieces of meat and found that the skewer rotates but the meat stays in the same position? It can be a bit frustrating when your chicken tikka is charring too much on the bottom and you can't get it to turn and cook the other side.

To fix this common problem, weave the skewer through the meat, don't just stick it straight through. By weaving it a few times through each piece of meat, it will be much more secure on the skewer and will rotate with the skewer when you want it to. This also applies to cuts of meat like lamb chops and bone-in chicken.

AFGHANI CHICKEN KEBABS
SERVES 4-6

I first tried Afghani kebabs in Mumbai and now I make them all the time at my home barbecues. When I cook chicken tikka kebabs, I like to make a few different marinades for a variety of colours and flavours. Cook these yellow-coloured kebabs up along with some red tandoori chicken tikka kebabs using the marinade on page 53 and deep green cafreal chicken tikka kebabs using the marinade on page 14 and you will have the ultimate kebab feast! Or just cook up some of these mouth-watering kebabs on their own – you won't be disappointed. Afghani chicken kebabs obviously made their way to India from Afghanistan, but they are hugely popular around the world. They are usually not spicy but if you prefer, you could add some minced chillies and/or more chilli powder to the mix.

PREP TIME: 15 MINS, PLUS MARINATING TIME
COOKING TIME: 15 MINS

900g (2lb) chicken breasts or thighs, cut into bite-size pieces
Melted ghee, for basting

FOR THE FIRST MARINADE
1 tsp shop-bought mint sauce (I use Colman's)
3 tbsp double (heavy) cream
Juice of 1 lemon
1 tsp salt, plus extra to taste

FOR THE SECOND MARINADE
2 tbsp garlic and ginger paste (see page 169)
2 tbsp gram (chickpea) flour
200g (generous ¾ cup) Greek yoghurt, whisked
1 tbsp ground almonds
1 tsp garam masala (see page 168)
1 tsp Kashmiri chilli powder
1 tsp ground turmeric
1 tsp dried fenugreek leaves (kasoori methi)
Handful of coriander (cilantro), finely chopped
2 tbsp mustard oil

Put the chicken pieces in a bowl, add the ingredients for the first marinade and rub well into the meat. Let sit for about 20 minutes while you prepare the second marinade.

Whisk together all of the second marinade ingredients until smooth. Cover the chicken pieces with this marinade, rubbing it right into the flesh, then cover and put in the fridge to marinate for 1 hour, or overnight – the longer the better.

Prepare a hot direct heat fire (see page 10). When the coals are white-hot and it is uncomfortable to hold your hand 5cm (2in) above cooking height for more than 2 seconds, you're ready to cook. Skewer the marinated chicken, weaving the skewer through the chicken at least twice. Don't simply stick the skewer through or the chicken will turn when you try to rotate the kebabs.

Grill over the hot coals for about 5 minutes, or until lightly charred, then flip the skewers to cook the other side. Rotate from time to time so that the chicken cooks evenly. When the chicken is almost cooked through, baste with the ghee. Serve hot, sprinkled with a little salt.

CHICKEN SHASHLIK
SERVES 6

Chicken shashlik is a hugely popular kebab and one of the easiest to prepare. You want a good combination of sweet, sour, savoury and spicy in the marinade, so it's best to try it and decide for yourself if you want to adjust the flavouring. This recipe also works well with pork, or if you want a vegetarian shashlik, try cubed paneer.

PREP TIME: 10 MINS, PLUS MARINATING TIME
COOKING TIME: 15 MINS

900g (2lb) boneless and skinless chicken thighs, cut into bite-size pieces
2 tomatoes, quartered
2 red onions, quartered and divided into thick petals
1 red (bell) pepper, cut into bite-size pieces
1 yellow (bell) pepper, cut into bite-size pieces
Green chutney, roasted onion raita or red chilli sauce, to serve (see pages 161–162)

FOR THE MARINADE
3 tbsp garlic, ginger and chilli paste (see page 169)
3 tbsp distilled white vinegar
Juice of 1 lemon
1 tsp garam masala (see page 168)
1 tsp Kashmiri chilli powder (more or less to taste)
½ tsp ground cumin
3 tbsp light soy sauce (see Note)
3 tbsp ketchup
1 tbsp Dijon mustard
4 tbsp finely chopped coriander (cilantro)
Salt and freshly ground black pepper, to taste

Combine all of the marinade ingredients apart from the coriander (cilantro) and salt and pepper in a bowl and whisk together. Season to taste and then stir in the finely chopped coriander. Add the chicken and veggies and stir to ensure everything is well coated. Leave to marinate for 30–60 minutes while you fire up your barbecue.

Prepare a direct heat fire (see page 10). When the coals are white-hot and it is uncomfortable to hold your hand 5cm (2in) above cooking height for more than 2 seconds, you're ready to cook. Prepare your kebabs by skewering alternate pieces of chicken and vegetables. Place the chicken shashlik kebabs on the grill over the hottest part of the fire and turn regularly so that they cook evenly. After 10–15 minutes, the chicken will be cooked through and you will have nice char marks in places on the meat and vegetables.

I like to serve these with coriander chutney, onion raita and/or a good chilli sauce.

NOTE
Some brands of soy sauce contain gluten. Use a gluten-free version if you need this dish to be gluten-free.

CHICKEN SEEKH KEBABS
SERVES 4

These juicy chicken kebabs can also be made with minced (ground) turkey. If purchasing your meat from a butcher, ask them to finely mince chicken thighs as they have the most flavour. Chicken seekh kebabs can be a bit dry, which is why I add rendered beef or lamb fat to mine. You can make your own or just purchase beef or lamb dripping. The dripping not only makes the kebabs juicy but also helps to keep the chicken on the skewers. You can use this same mixture to make chicken patties for burgers, or try this mix in my lamb and chicken seekh kebabs on page 23. Before cooking, take a look at my advice on achieving the perfect seekh kebabs on page 39.

PREP TIME: 15 MINS, PLUS CHILLING TIME
COOKING TIME: 10 MINS

1 red onion, roughly chopped
6 garlic cloves, crushed
2.5cm (1in) piece of ginger, peeled and roughly chopped
6 green bird's eye chillies, roughly chopped
2 tbsp chopped coriander (cilantro), optional
1kg (2lb 4oz) minced (ground) chicken
4 tbsp beef or lamb dripping, homemade or shop-bought, at room temperature
1 tbsp ground cumin
1 tbsp ground coriander
1 tsp garam masala (see page 168)
1½ tsp salt
2 tbsp Kashmiri chilli powder (more or less to taste)
3 tbsp melted ghee, plus extra for greasing
Rice or naans and salad, to serve
Green chutney (see page 162), to serve

Put the onion into a food processor and blend to a coarse paste. Scrape the blended onion into a porous dish cloth and wrap it tightly into a ball. Twist the cloth, extracting as much moisture from the onion as you can. Set aside.

Next add the garlic, ginger, chillies and coriander (cilantro), if using, to the food processor and blend finely. This could also be done by hand with a knife, or in a pestle and mortar. Set aside.

Put the minced (ground) chicken and the dripping into a food processor and blend until smooth. I usually do this in batches. Transfer to a large bowl, add the blended onion, garlic, ginger, chilli and coriander paste and all the remaining ingredients, apart from the ghee. Mix well with your hands to combine. Cover and put in the fridge to chill for at least 2 hours, or overnight.

When ready to cook, prepare a multi-level direct heat fire (see page 10). Take a ball of the chicken mixture and begin forming it around a lightly greased skewer. I have given detailed instructions on how to do this on page 23.

When the coals are white-hot and it is uncomfortable to hold your hand 5cm (2in) above the grill for more than 2 seconds, you're ready to cook. Lay your skewered seekh kebabs over the fire and cook, rotating them from time to time so that they cook evenly. When almost cooked through, baste with the ghee. The cooking time will vary depending on the size of your kebabs, but should take about 10 minutes, or until the internal temperature reaches 75°C (165°F). Serve with rice or naans, salad and green chutney.

From left to right: Peshawari namak mandi (page 44); chicken seekh kebabs; chicken shashlik (page 41); vegetable skewers (page 32)

PESHAWARI NAMAK MANDI
SERVES 4

This lamb kebab recipe stems from north-western Pakistan, bordering Afghanistan. The area is known for its simple but delicious cuisine, which calls for limited spicing and relies heavily on top quality, fatty meats for flavour. Unlike other parts of Pakistan and North India where ghee is used a lot in recipes, in this area rendered lamb or mutton fat is used to cook the meat so succulently. Don't let the minimal ingredients stop you from trying this one! My wife was amazed by the flavour and was very surprised when I told her how simple it was. The meat from this recipe is also an excellent substitute for the chicken in my chicken karahi recipe (see page 95).

PREP TIME: 10 MINS
COOKING TIME: 25 MINS

900g (2lb) lamb or mutton leg meat, fat trimmed and cut into slightly larger than bite-size pieces
300g (10½oz) lamb fat, cut into pieces the same size as the meat
Approx. 2 tbsp fine sea salt
Salad, chapatis, raita and chutney, to serve

Put the lamb or mutton and fat into a bowl and sprinkle generously with salt. Mix well so that the meat is equally coated in salt. You should do this at least 1 hour before cooking or the day before if you can (the longer the better).

Set up your barbecue for medium-high direct heat cooking (see page 10). Slide the meat onto skewers, leaving a little space between each piece. Then skewer the fat onto another skewer (it's fine for these pieces of fat to touch).

When you can only place your hand at cooking height over the coals for 3–4 seconds before it gets too hot, you're ready to cook. Place the skewered meat and fat over the fire and turn every minute. This might sound a lot, but you are making up for the lack of ingredients so trust me here. Open yourself a cold beer and continue cooking and turning for 20 minutes. As the fat chunks cook, they will begin to release dripping fat. Take the fat skewer and use it to baste the meat chunks. Return the fat to the heat and repeat often. Doing this will not only keep the meat juicy but it will also cause some of the salt to drip off into the fire so that the finished lamb isn't too salty.

The meat is ready when it is super tender and lightly charred. Chop the fat finely and serve with the meat, along with salad, chapatis and a raita or chutney.

LAMB SEEKH KEBABS
SERVES 4

You might know that I featured a lamb seekh kebab recipe in my first cookbook, which was actually my go-to recipe for many years. Well, this is my go-to recipe now, for no other reason than I like to vary my recipes from time to time. Before cooking, take a look at my advice on achieving the perfect seekh kebabs on page 39. The most important thing to remember is that this meat mixture tastes great. If cooking on a skewer sounds too fussy, go ahead and cook the kebabs in sausage or patty shapes directly on the grill.

PREP TIME: 25 MINS, PLUS CHILLING TIME
COOKING TIME: 25 MINS

1 red onion, finely chopped
5 garlic cloves, crushed
4 green bird's eye chillies
2 tbsp finely chopped mint leaves
2 tbsp finely chopped coriander (cilantro)
1kg (2lb 4oz) 20% fat finely minced (ground) lamb
1 tsp salt
1 tbsp Kashmiri chilli powder (more or less to taste)
2 tsp ground coriander
1 tsp ground cumin
½ tsp ground black pepper
3 tbsp melted ghee, plus extra for greasing
Green chutney (see page 162), to serve

Put the onion into a food processor and blend to a coarse paste. Scrape the blended onion into a porous dish cloth and wrap it tightly into a ball. Twist the cloth, extracting as much moisture from the onion as you can. Set aside.

Next add the garlic, chillies, mint and coriander (cilantro) to the food processor and blend finely. This could also be done by hand with a knife, or in a pestle and mortar. Put the minced (ground) lamb into a bowl, then add the garlic, chilli and herb mixture along with the onion, salt chilli powder and ground spices. Knead it until well combined, then cover and put in the coldest part of the fridge for 2 hours, or overnight.

When ready to cook, prepare a multi-level direct heat fire (see page 10). Place a bowl of water next to the meat mixture and skewers. Wet your hand, take a ball of meat and begin squeezing it down a lightly greased skewer into a sausage shape. Don't be afraid to really squeeze! You should see your finger indentations on the kebab. Ensure that it is tightly packed on the skewer with no bits hanging off. This might take some practice so just go with care and you'll get there. Give the kebab a good shake. If the meat is falling off, keep squeezing until it doesn't.

When the coals are white-hot and it is uncomfortable to hold your hand 5cm (2in) above the grill for more than 2 seconds, place a couple of skewers over the hottest part of the fire and start cooking, turning the kebabs regularly so that the meat cooks evenly. As they brown, baste the kebabs with the ghee and then move them to a cooler part of the grill and put a couple more skewers over the high heat. Repeat until all the kebabs are cooked through.

Serve immediately with green chutney (or the sauce of your choice).

NOTE
It is important that the meat is finely minced for this recipe. You can do this by hand or use a food processor, or otherwise ask your butcher to run the meat through the mincer about three times.

CHEESY BATTERED SEEKH KEBABS
SERVES 4-6

If you like cheese and kebabs, you're going to love this one! You can use any cheese you like to fill these delicious kebabs. The most common cheese to use is processed yellow cheese but you can fill them with Stilton, chilli Cheddar – anything really. It is essential that you have large skewers to make these, as shown in the photograph, but if you don't, go ahead and just add cheese to the lamb seekh kebab mixture and it will still be very good.

PREP TIME: 30 MINS
COOKING TIME: 30 MINS

1 batch lamb seekh kebab mixture (see page 45)
Approx. 150g (5½oz) cheese of your choice
75g (5 tbsp) plain (all-purpose) flour
1 tsp baking powder
75g (5 tbsp) cornflour (cornstarch)
1 large egg
1 tsp lemon juice
2 tsp garlic and ginger paste (see page 169)
Rapeseed (canola) oil, for frying
Raita or chilli sauce, to serve

Use the lamb seekh kebab mixture to form kebabs (see page 45). Once formed on the skewers, give them a shake to ensure the meat is secure and won't fall off.

Prepare a multi-level direct heat fire (see page 10). When the coals are white-hot and it is uncomfortable to hold your hand 5cm (2in) above the grill for more than 2 seconds, you're ready to cook. Place the skewers directly over the coals and cook for about 5 minutes until browned on one side. Rotate to cook the other side and then continue rotating until nicely charred all round.

Once cooked, transfer the kebabs from the grill to a clean surface and leave to cool, then remove them from the skewers. Cut each one into 3 pieces, then fill the holes with the cheese. You might need to help it through with the skewer if using processed cheese. When using other varieties, I simply cut slices of cheese that are the same size in thickness as the skewer hole and slide them in.

Next make the batter by whisking together the remaining ingredients (apart from the oil) with 300ml (1¼ cups) water until you have a smooth, thick paste.

Half-fill a large saucepan with rapeseed (canola) oil and heat to 170°C (340°F). If you don't have an oil thermometer, the oil is hot enough when a small bit of the batter added to it sizzles to the top immediately.

Dip the filled seekh kebabs in the batter and then lower them gently into the hot oil. Fry for a couple of minutes, or until starting to turn golden brown. Serve immediately while the cheese inside is still hot, with your favourite raita or chilli sauce.

Top: Lamb seekh kebabs (page 45)
Bottom: Cheesy battered seekh kebabs

FLATTENED BEEF KEBABS
SERVES 4-6

I was introduced to these while studying in northern Germany by my friend Ramin from Iran. I loved them! The accompanying crispy rice dish was the perfect side. One weekend, we went hiking with a group of friends, along with my future wife, and set up camp by the sea. We cooked these kebabs and rice on the beach and chased it all down with lots of cold German lager. What a night! These kebabs, often called chelo kebabs, were introduced to India by the Moguls and I was really happy to find them again, served with saffron crispy rice, when I last visited India. If you have wide, flat metal skewers, this is a good recipe for them.

PREP TIME: 30 MINS, PLUS CHILLING TIME
COOKING TIME: 20 MINS

2 onions, roughly chopped
1kg (2lb 4oz) 20% fat minced (ground) beef
3 tbsp garlic, ginger and chilli paste (see page 169)
1 tbsp ground cumin
1 tbsp ground coriander
1 tbsp garam masala (see page 168)
1 tsp salt, plus extra to taste
1½ tsp ground black pepper
3 tbsp melted ghee, plus extra for greasing
8 vine tomatoes
8 shallots, peeled but left whole
2 tbsp rapeseed (canola) oil
Crispy saffron rice (see page 149), to serve

Put the onions into a food processor and blend to a coarse paste. Scrape the blended onion into a porous dish cloth and wrap it tightly into a ball. Twist the cloth, extracting as much moisture from the onion as you can. Set aside.

Put the meat into the food processor and blend until you have a smooth, paste-like mixture. You might need to do this in batches. Transfer the meat to a large bowl and add the onion, along with the garlic, ginger and chilli paste, spices and salt and pepper. Knead until well combined. For this recipe, it is essential that the meat is very cold, so cover and put in the fridge for about 1 hour, or for best results, overnight.

When ready to cook, prepare a multi-level direct heat fire (see page 10). Place a bowl of water next to your skewers and then take a large handful of the meat mixture and work it into a pool-ball-sized ball. Slide this onto a lightly greased skewer and begin squeezing it onto the skewer with a wet hand. Once the meat is secure on the skewer, make pronounced indentations with your fingers. Repeat with the rest of the meat.

When the coals are white-hot and it is uncomfortable to hold your hand 5cm (2in) above the grill for more than 2 seconds, you're ready to cook. Place the kebabs over the coals and cook for about a minute before turning. Continue turning until nicely charred on both sides, basting from time to time with the melted ghee.

Meanwhile, coat the tomatoes and shallots with the rapeseed (canola) oil and season with salt. Once the kebabs have cooked to your liking, transfer them to the cooler part of the grill to smoke a little and skewer the tomatoes and shallots. Cook these over a high heat until charred and cooked through, which should only take about 5 minutes.

Serve the finished kebabs with the tomatoes, shallots and saffron rice – or whatever you think sounds good.

Left: Crispy saffron rice (page 149)
Right: Flattened beef kebabs

VEGGIE SEEKH KEBAB
SERVES 4-6

You can get really creative with vegetarian seekh kebabs. I suggest a few vegetables to use below but you're not limited to those! The most important ingredient in this recipe is the mashed potato. That and the cheese, if using, is what binds the kebabs together. Like all seekh kebabs, it is difficult at first to get these to stay on the skewers. If this is your first time attempting veggie seekh kebabs, you could start them off on a double layer of foil that has been oiled and placed directly over the grate. This will help them stay on the skewer – once a crust has formed you can remove the foil and then finish them off over the hot coals. With practice you won't need to do this but it is a good way to get started.

PREP TIME: 25 MINS, PLUS CHILLING TIME
COOKING TIME: 15 MINS

3 large floury potatoes, unpeeled
3 tbsp rapeseed (canola) oil or ghee
2 tsp cumin seeds
1 onion, finely chopped
2 tbsp garlic and ginger paste (see page 169)
5 green bird's eye chillies, finely chopped
70g (2½oz) cauliflower, roughly chopped
70g (2½oz) broccoli, roughly chopped
1 large carrot, roughly chopped
70g (2½oz) green (string) beans, roughly chopped
1 red (bell) pepper, roughly chopped
1 tsp dried red chilli flakes
1 tsp ground coriander
½ tsp ground turmeric
1 tsp Kashmiri chilli powder
Large handful of coriander (cilantro), roughly chopped
Small handful of mint leaves, roughly chopped
100g (3½oz) Cheddar or paneer cheese, grated (optional)
3 tbsp melted ghee, plus extra for greasing
Salt, to taste
Chutney, raita or chilli sauce, to serve

Put the potatoes in a saucepan and cover with water. Bring to a boil over a high heat and simmer until fork tender. Transfer to a plate to cool and then peel and mash them. Set aside.

Heat the oil or ghee in a large frying pan over a medium-high heat. When visibly hot, stir in the cumin seeds and fry for 30 seconds to infuse into the oil. Add the chopped onion and fry for about 3 minutes until soft and translucent. Then stir in the garlic and ginger paste and chopped chillies and fry for a further 30 seconds.

Add the cauliflower, broccoli, carrot, green (string) beans and red (bell) pepper to the pan and stir-fry until almost cooked through but not super soft. Stir in the chilli flakes and ground spices and fry for a further 30 seconds, then remove from the heat and allow to cool slightly.

Once cooled, transfer the vegetable mixture to a food processor and blend until you have a chunky paste – not smooth like mashed potato; you want to see little bits of vegetable. Mix the vegetables with the mashed potato, coriander (cilantro), mint and cheese, if using, and season to taste. Refrigerate for 30 minutes, or until cold.

Prepare a direct heat fire (see page 10). While the barbecue is heating up, start preparing your skewers. Place a bowl of water next to the skewers and with wet hands, take a pool-ball-sized ball of the potato mixture and slide it onto a lightly greased skewer. Squeeze it onto the skewer. As you do this, it will make its way down the skewer to form a sausage shape. The mixture should be evenly distributed on the skewer. Repeat with the remaining mixture.

When the coals are white-hot and it is uncomfortable to hold your hand 5cm (2in) above the grill for more than 2 seconds, you're ready to cook. Place the seekh kebabs over the coals and cook, turning regularly, until they are heated through and a light, crispy brown. Baste from time to time with the melted ghee.

Serve with chutney, raita and/or chilli sauce. These are also delicious wrapped in chapatis or naans with salad.

CHICKEN COOKED IN BANANA LEAVES
SERVES 4

I've cooked this the traditional way a few times. I dug a deep hole in my back garden and built a big charcoal fire in it. When the coals ashed over and were really hot, I placed my banana-leaf-and-foil-wrapped chicken on the coals and buried it with more burning coals and earth. My first attempt wasn't good. I dug the chicken out after 90 minutes, just in time to serve dinner. The coals were still quite hot, but the chicken was raw. The next time I tried it, I buried the chicken for 4½ hours and it was perfect. So, this method works and it offers people without an oven a good way of slowly cooking a chicken, but my barbecued method below is much faster and almost as good.

PREP TIME: 20 MINS
COOKING TIME: 1 HOUR

Banana leaves, to wrap the chicken
1.5kg (3lb 5oz) skinless whole chicken
Juice of 1 large lemon
1 tsp salt
2 tbsp garlic and ginger paste (see page 169)
4 tbsp melted ghee
2 tbsp Kashmiri chilli powder
2 tbsp ground cumin
2 tbsp ground coriander
1 tsp garam masala (see page 168)
1 tsp ground black pepper
1 lemon, thinly sliced
Rice, naans, chapatis, salad and chutneys, to serve

Wash the banana leaves with hot water and ensure there is no sand on them. Set aside. Score the chicken all over with a sharp knife. This will allow the marinade to really get in there and flavour the chicken. Rub the lemon juice, salt and garlic and ginger paste all over the chicken and set aside. Mix the melted ghee with the ground spices and rub this onto the chicken and inside the cavity, too. Wrap the chicken tightly in the banana leaves so that there are no holes and then wrap again with foil.

Set up your barbecue for indirect heat cooking (see page 9). You will probably need quite a lot of charcoal as the chicken will need to cook for 1 hour or more. Light the coals and, when ready, cover the barbecue and open the top and bottom vents completely. You're aiming for a cooking temperature of 180–200°C (355–400°F). Once this heat is achieved, you can maintain it by adjusting the top and bottom vents (see page 10).

Place the tightly wrapped chicken on the cooking grate over the side with no coals and close the lid. Cook for 1 hour, or until the chicken reaches an internal temperature of 75°C (165°F). Transfer to a cutting board and allow to rest for about 20 minutes. Unwrap and carve to serve. This chicken is delicious served with rice, naans, chapatis, salad and chutneys.

TANDOORI ROAST CHICKEN
SERVES 4

This recipe is a little different to most tandoori chicken recipes you'll find out there. First of all, I leave the chicken skin on just as I did in the beer can chicken recipe in *The Curry Guy Easy*. Why? Because crispy chicken skin is so good! Then I simply use my go-to tandoori marinade. It's like the one you find in those jars at the shop, but better. I also don't use the yoghurt that usually goes into a tandoori marinade as it isn't needed when cooking chicken like this. Butterflying the bird gets a faster, more even cook with juicier results. It's an excellent marinade for chicken tikka too, with or without yoghurt.

PREP TIME: 15 MINS, PLUS MARINATING TIME
COOKING TIME: 1 HOUR

1.5kg (3lb 5oz) whole chicken
70ml (¼ cup) melted ghee mixed with 1 tsp salt

FOR THE TANDOORI MARINADE
1 tbsp ground cumin
1 tbsp ground coriander
1 tbsp tandoori masala (see page 167)
1 tbsp garam masala (see page 168)
1 tsp ground turmeric
1 tsp amchoor (dried mango powder)
1 tbsp Kashmiri chilli powder (more or less to taste, or mild paprika)
2 tbsp garlic, ginger and chilli paste (see page 169)
1 tsp ground black pepper
1 tsp salt
3 tbsp lemon juice
1 tbsp distilled white vinegar
4 tbsp rapeseed (canola) oil

Place the chicken in an upright sitting position on a cutting board. Using a sharp knife, slice down between the breasts to butterfly. Many people remove the backbone to butterfly chicken rather than doing it in this way, but I find that the chicken lies flatter when cooking if you slice between the breasts. Lay the chicken on the cutting board breast side up and press down hard all over to flatten.

Next, whisk together all of the marinade ingredients, adding just enough water to make a smooth paste – about 3 tablespoons.

I usually slide a couple of fingers under the skin all over the breasts, legs and thighs so that I can rub the meat with the marinade as well as the skin on top. This really gets the flavour into the chicken. Rub the marinade all over the chicken and under the skin if you like, then cover and leave to marinate in the fridge for at least 1 hour, or overnight.

When ready to cook, set up your barbecue for indirect heat roasting (see page 9). Your target temperature is 250°C (480°F) or there abouts. If using a normal kettle barbecue, be sure to place a drip tray with a little water in it on the cooler side opposite the coals. This isn't necessary if using a ceramic barbecue.

Place the butterflied chicken breast side up on the side of the barbecue without any coals and cook until the internal temperature is 75°C (165°F). This should take 45–60 minutes. Baste the chicken from time to time with the melted ghee until it is all used up.

I recommend serving this with masala garlic fries (see page 146) or karahi naans (see page 153). This tandoori chicken is also so good teamed with green chutney (see page 162).

NOTE
It is up to you how much chopped green chilli you add to your garlic and ginger paste; if you like plenty of heat, don't hold back!

(GF)

SPICY WHOLE CHICKEN ON A SKEWER
SERVES 2–3

Like so many of the recipes in this book, this one stems from Pakistan. They seem to love their meat in the north. This dish is called chicken sajji. I've been told that originally it was cooked with a whole goat but nowadays it's made with chicken, too, as it's cheaper and of course more practical to serve at a restaurant or food stall. The original marinade was simply salt and perhaps a bit of vinegar but these days it is spiced up. This is a great recipe for campfire cooking. You just need a couple of skewers and a good fire. Cook just one chicken or double the marinade and cook a few at the same time. If you have a rotisserie, you could also cheat and use it for this. This might seem a ridiculously long cook to some but that smoky, succulent chicken is worth the wait!

PREP TIME: 20 MINS. PLUS MARINATING TIME
COOKING TIME: 4 HOURS

4 tbsp dried red chilli flakes
1½ tbsp salt
1 tbsp ground coriander
1 tbsp ground cumin
3 tbsp garlic, ginger and chilli paste (see page 169)
90ml (⅓ cup) distilled white vinegar
1.5kg (3lb 5oz) whole chicken
Lemon wedges, to serve
Green salad, to serve
Crispy saffron rice (see page 149), to serve

Combine the chilli flakes, 1 tablespoon of the salt, the ground coriander, cumin, garlic, ginger and chilli paste and 5 tablespoons of the vinegar in a bowl. Stir well to make a thick paste and set aside.

Carefully run your fingers beneath the skin of the chicken to separate it from the meat and make a few shallow slits in the flesh of the breasts and thighs. Rub the marinade into the flesh and inside the carcass, reserving about 2 tablespoons for later. Finally, rub the remaining salt and vinegar into the skin. Cover and put in the fridge to marinate for at least 2 hours, or overnight.

When ready to cook, build a log fire using kiln-dried logs (see page 9). I use a combination of oak and apple. Skewer the chicken by running a large skewer through one of the thighs and then straight through the centre and out one of the breasts. Tie the legs together tightly so that the chicken doesn't slide down the skewer while cooking (you could also secure the chicken in place with a potato as shown in the photograph opposite). Stick the skewer in the ground right next to the fire. The chicken should stand close enough to the flame so that it cooks and smokes. You can also move some of the coals right under the skewered chicken for additional heat.

Now it's time to grab a beer and relax. At this stage, you are both cooking and smoking the chicken. You can do that for a few hours if you want or speed it all up by adding more logs and moving the chicken closer to the fire. Chicken sajji is normally cooked low and slow and then moved to a position right over the hot fire to finish it off when you are ready to eat. You could cook this recipe in just over an hour or let it cook much longer for even more delicious smoky flavour.

When you move the chicken to directly over the coals, baste it with the remaining marinade. The skin should begin to char and burn off; most of it is rubbed off but any remaining will taste pretty good. Serve with lemon wedges, a green salad and crispy saffron rice.

ROASTED RABBIT
SERVES 2-3

This marinade, though quite simple, is perfect for roasted rabbit, which is similar in flavour to chicken. When teamed with the melted ghee, which is brushed over the rabbit as it cooks, it is so good. The marinade used in the tandoori roast chicken recipe on page 53 also works really well with rabbit cooked this way.

PREP TIME: 15 MINS, PLUS MARINATING TIME
COOKING TIME: 1½ HOURS

1 whole wild rabbit
70ml (¼ cup) melted ghee
Pilau rice and salad, to serve

FOR THE MARINADE
3 tbsp rapeseed (canola) oil
¼ small red onion
2 garlic cloves
1 tbsp garlic and ginger paste (see page 169)
5 tbsp finely chopped coriander (cilantro)
2 tsp Kashmiri chilli powder
Juice of 1 lime
Salt and freshly ground black pepper, to taste

Butterfly the rabbit by using kitchen shears (or a sharp knife) to cut the underside open from neck to tail end, then placing it belly side down on a cutting board and pressing it down with your hands to flatten a little. Using a sharp knife, make shallow slits every 2.5cm (1in) down the body and legs on both sides.

Blend all the marinade ingredients together in a pestle and mortar or small food processor and rub it all over the rabbit, making sure you get it right into the slits you cut. Marinate for at least 1 hour, or overnight.

When ready to cook, fire up your barbecue for roasting (see page 9). When the heat reaches a steady 180°C (355°F) you're ready to cook. If using a kettle-style barbecue, place a drip pan on the cooler side of the barbecue with a little water in it. (This isn't necessary if using a ceramic barbecue.) Place the rabbit, belly side down, on the cool side of the barbecue over the drip pan and close the lid. You will need to roast the rabbit until the internal temperature reaches 71°C (160°F). This will take about 1½ hours. From time to time while the rabbit is roasting, lift the lid and quickly baste it with the melted ghee. You can just place the ghee in a small pan or metal cup next to the rabbit on the grill to keep it warm.

Once cooked, remove the rabbit from the heat and allow to rest somewhere warm for 10 minutes before serving. I like to eat this with pilau rice and a green salad.

SMOKED AND SEARED DUCK BREAST WITH BUTTERNUT SQUASH

SERVES 4

Putting the duck and squash right in the embers of your fire is a delicious way to cook this recipe. You can use charcoal here but I recommend getting at least a couple of kiln-dried oak logs to cook the duck on. The smoky flavour is amazing! Don't feel like you have to do everything at once. The squash can be cooked in the embers and set aside. You can then cook the duck on the logs and finish by crisping up the skin in a frying pan. You will need two pans for this recipe.

PREP TIME: 10 MINS
COOKING TIME: 30 MINS

1 butternut squash, unpeeled and cut into about 10 pieces
1 tbsp butter
2 tbsp rapeseed (canola) oil or coconut oil
1 tsp black mustard seeds
20 fresh or frozen curry leaves
½ tsp garam masala (see page 168)
4 large duck breasts (approx. 180g/6oz each), skin scored
Tamarind sauce, to taste (see page 167 or use shop-bought)
Salt and freshly ground black pepper, to taste

Prepare a direct heat fire (see page 10). Once the coals are good and hot, add a couple of oak logs so that they can begin burning. Place the pieces of squash right down in the embers. Allow to char and then turn. Keep turning until blackened on the outside and about 80% cooked through. Transfer to a cutting board and chop into bite-size pieces.

Place a frying pan right down on the coals and add the butter and oil. When visibly hot, stir in the mustard seeds and when they begin to pop, add the curry leaves. When the leaves start to crackle a bit, stir in the chopped squash and cook for a few minutes until cooked through and caramelized. Season with salt to taste and sprinkle with the garam masala, then remove from the direct heat and keep warm.

Season the duck breasts generously with salt and pepper and place them, meat side down on a hot, smouldering log or large piece of lumpwood charcoal (see page 9). Leave them there until the duck is about a quarter of the way cooked through – this will take roughly 20 minutes, but of course that depends on the heat of your logs. Next place a frying pan on the coals and lay the duck breasts in it, skin side down. As the pan heats up, the fat will begin to render out of the skin. Keep frying until the skin is crisp and nicely browned. I like to serve farmed duck medium rare and still pink in the centre as I find it becomes a bit dry when overcooked. If you have a meat thermometer, you should aim for an internal heat of 55°C (130°F). Transfer to a cutting board and allow to rest for about 7 minutes. As the duck rests, the temperature will continue to rise to about 60°C (140°F). Perfect!

Drizzle the tamarind sauce over a plate, then slice the duck breasts diagonally into about 8 pieces each and place them on top of the tamarind sauce. Serve with the caramelized squash.

GF

SMOKY MASALA BRISKET
SERVES 10–12

I've cooked more briskets over the years than I could possibly count. There is a big debate as to which cooking method gets the best result. Some people slow-cook theirs uncovered for the whole cook; this achieves a brilliant flavour that is hard to beat. Others wrap their brisket halfway through the cook in butcher's paper or foil. Using foil achieves a juicier brisket than unwrapped brisket but still gets a respectable bark on the outside. Smoking brisket comes with a lean 'flat' end and a 'point' end. Ask your butcher for the 'point' with the fat trimmed to a 5mm (¼in) thickness – it's by far the juicier cut.

PREP TIME: 10 MINS
COOKING TIME: 8 HOURS

3 tbsp all-purpose rub (see page 169), or just salt and pepper
70ml (¼ cup) melted ghee
2.5kg (5½lb) smoking brisket (not rolled!)
½ batch my all-purpose BBQ sauce (see page 166), optional

Set up your barbecue for indirect heat cooking (see page 9) and whisk together the spice rub and the ghee. Using a small, sharp knife, make incisions all over the brisket and then coat it with the spice mixture.

Once your coals are good and hot, move them all over to one side of your barbecue and place a drip pan on the side with no coals (this isn't necessary if you have a ceramic barbecue). Put the cooking grate on top and then place the spice-coated brisket on the grate over the drip pan, fat side up. Put the lid on your barbecue and aim for a cooking temperature of 110°C (225°F). Check this often, as the cooking temperature is important! If the temperature is too high, close the vent holes slightly. If it's not hot enough, open the vents up a little.

Once you have the barbecue burning at a steady 110°C (225°F) or there abouts, check the temperature every 45 minutes to 1 hour. Start a few briquettes burning in a chimney starter or similar so that they are ready. You will need them. If the temperature cools down to 100°C (210°F), add a couple of hot briquettes to the coals in the barbecue, close the lid and open the vent holes a bit. Adjust the vents and repeat this process as required.

After the brisket has been smoking for 3–4 hours at this temperature, you will have achieved a super smoky and delicious brisket. You're not done yet though! Wrap the brisket loosely in foil, being sure to press the foil together so that no steam can escape, and continue cooking for another 3–4 hours at 120°C (250°F), or until the meat reaches an internal temperature of 82°C (180°F). Remember, this is barbecue so cooking times can and probably will vary. It could take you a couple more hours of cooking so please don't rush this.

As with most barbecued meats, brisket will benefit from resting before slicing. I place mine in an ice chest and cover it with towels before replacing the lid and let it sit there for about an hour or two.

Once ready, transfer the meat in the foil to a board. Open it up and pour the cooking juices from the foil into a pan; keep warm. Slice the meat thinly against the grain and place on a serving dish. Drizzle with the cooking juices and serve. I recommend serving with dipping bowls of my all-purpose BBQ sauce.

REVERSE-SEARED TOMAHAWK STEAKS
SERVES 2–4

For me, a tomahawk steak needs to be smoky in flavour, nicely charred and medium rare in the centre. That's just me, though; you might prefer yours rare or well done so adjust the instructions below to achieve your perfect steak. Remember, you want to cook this by temperature and not time, so having a good meat thermometer for this recipe is a good idea.

PREP TIME: 15 MINS
COOKING TIME: 30 MINS

2 x 900g (2lb) tomahawk steaks
3–4 tbsp all-purpose rub (see page 169)
Oil, for brushing

Rub the steaks all over with the all-purpose rub. It is important to do this at least 1 hour before cooking but overnight will achieve even better results. When ready to cook, set up your barbecue for indirect heat cooking (see page 9). If using a normal kettle barbecue, place a drip pan with a little water in it opposite the coals. This isn't necessary if using a ceramic barbecue. When the barbecue has reached a steady cooking temperature of between 110°C (225°F) and 120°C (245°F), you're ready to get cooking. I tend to aim for the lower temperature for a longer cook.

Cover the long bone extending from the tomahawk steaks with foil and place them directly on the grill over the drip pan or opposite the coals and close the lid. You can maintain the cooking heat by adjusting the top and bottom vents (see page 10). Allow to cook until the steaks have reached an internal temperature of 47°C (116°F), then transfer to a plate, cover loosely with foil and leave to rest. The residual heat will continue to cook the steaks before you finish them back on the grill.

Meanwhile, spread your coals out in the barbecue and add more charcoal if needed. You might like to get some charcoal fired up in a chimney starter so that it's ready to add if you need it. At this point, you can open both the top and bottom vents wide open to get the grill as hot as possible.

When the steaks have rested and you're ready to finish cooking, open the lid and lightly brush the cooking grate with a little oil. I usually place the steaks back on the grill when they reach 53°C (128°F) for medium rare. Place the steaks directly over the hottest part of the fire and cook on one side for about a minute until nicely charred (flare-ups are fine as the steaks are only over the fire for a short time), then flip the steaks using tongs and char the other side. This generally achieves my preferred and recommended internal temperature of 56°C (133°F). Transfer to a plate to rest for about 10 minutes before slicing.

These steaks are awesome just as they are, although I like to serve them with the tomato chutney on page 164. Another delicious option is the avocado chutney on page 89, either as is or blended with a couple of tablespoons of Greek yoghurt until smooth.

HANGER STEAK WITH SPICED BONE MARROW
SERVES 2–4

Hanger steak – so called because it hangs near the diaphragm of the cow – is becoming increasingly popular these days. The muscle cut isn't used by the animal so it's tender like fillet but with more flavour. It does come with a lot of gristle, sinew and fat but a good butcher will remove this for you – you do need to start with a clean piece of meat for this recipe. Although this cut is good marinated, here it is cooked only with salt and lime juice and then served with deliciously spiced bone marrow. You will need a frying pan for the bone marrow canoes.

PREP TIME: 15 MINS
COOKING TIME: 5–10 MINS

Juice of 2 limes, plus extra lime wedges to serve
1 hanger steak (approx. 1kg/2lb 4oz), sliced down the centre into two long steaks
1 tbsp rapeseed (canola) oil
Salt, to taste

FOR THE SPICED BONE MARROW
2 handfuls of coriander (cilantro), finely chopped
6 garlic cloves, finely chopped
1 tsp Kashmiri chilli powder
1 tsp ground cumin
1 tbsp rapeseed (canola) oil
1 tsp salt
1 tsp coarsely ground black pepper
4 canoe-cut marrow bones

Squeeze the lime juice over the steaks, drizzle with the oil and season generously with salt. This should be done at least 1 hour before cooking or up to 10 hours for even better results. When ready to cook, prepare a direct heat fire (see page 10). While the coals are heating up, mix together the coriander (cilantro), garlic, chilli powder, cumin, oil, salt and pepper in a bowl. Set aside.

When the coals are white-hot and it is uncomfortable to hold your hand 5cm (2in) above the grill for more than 2 seconds, you're ready to cook. Lightly brush the cooking grate with oil and then place the bone marrow bones on the grate, cut side down, for 30 seconds. Turn over and continue roasting the bones by moving them from side to side. As the bone marrow cooks, it will begin to break away from the bone and melt. When this happens, transfer the bones to a frying pan to continue cooking until the bone marrow is soft and oozing deliciousness. Brush each generously with the coriander mixture and wrap in foil to keep warm while you cook the steaks.

Place the steaks on the hot grill and cook for about 5 minutes, turning every 30 seconds. I know that sounds like a lot of fuss but they cook better that way. Cook the steaks until they reach an internal temperature of 50°C (122°F) for rare or 56°C (133°F) for medium. Transfer to a cutting board and allow to rest for a few minutes. If the bone marrow has cooled too much, return to the pan and place back on the grill to heat up.

Slice the steaks against the grain and serve with the bone marrow. You can dip the meat into the hot marrow or scoop it out and let it melt on top of the steaks. Serve with lime wedges for squeezing over.

BUTTERFLIED LAMB RAAN
SERVES 6

I'm a big fan of a good lamb raan (leg) on the bone but I love cooking butterflied leg of lamb too, so I decided to give this a go. In India, raan is always cooked slowly until well done and tender, more often than not because it isn't lamb being served but mutton or goat, which needs a longer cooking time. I have given this hugely popular dish my own treatment, grilling the deliciously marinated and butterflied leg of lamb until medium rare, so that it is still quite pink and juicy inside. If you'd like to try a more traditional raan, give the goat raan on page 108 a try!

PREP TIME: 20 MINS, PLUS MARINATING TIME
COOKING TIME: 1 HOUR

1 leg of lamb (approx. 2kg/4½lb), surface fat removed and butterflied
10 garlic cloves, thinly sliced
2 tbsp garlic and ginger paste (see page 169)
2 tbsp lemon juice
2 tbsp distilled white vinegar
3 tbsp melted ghee
Sea salt
Green chutney (see page 162), to serve

FOR THE MARINADE
4 tbsp mustard oil, brought to smoking point in a pan and then allowed to cool
6 green bird's eye chillies, roughly chopped
1 tbsp ground cumin
1 tbsp ground coriander
1 tbsp tandoori masala (see page 167)
4 tbsp Kashmiri chilli powder (more or less to taste)
1 tbsp freshly ground black pepper
6 generous tbsp crispy fried onions (shop-bought is fine)
1 tbsp salt, plus extra to taste
2 tbsp distilled white vinegar
2 tbsp lemon juice
2 tbsp garlic and ginger paste (see page 169)
500g (2 cups) Greek yoghurt, whisked

Place the butterflied leg of lamb on a clean surface and try to flatten it some more by making slits across the meat. This will also give you more surface area for the fantastic marinade. Now take a sharp knife and make holes all over the meat. Stick the garlic slices deep into the holes and then rub the meat all over with the garlic and ginger paste, lemon juice and vinegar. Season generously with sea salt.

Next put all of the marinade ingredients except for the yoghurt into a food processor and blend to a smooth paste. Put this paste in a bowl with the yoghurt and whisk until it is well combined. Rub this marinade all over the meat, being sure to get it right into the slits you made. Cover tightly with cling film (plastic wrap) and place in the fridge for 24–48 hours, the longer the better (but yes, you can marinate for a shorter time if needs must).

When ready to cook, set up your barbecue for indirect heat cooking (see page 9). Close the lid and open the air vents until you reach a cooking temperature of about 190°C (375°F). I use a Kamado Joe barbecue, which has an indirect plate that can be placed under the meat, but if you don't have that feature, just place a drip pan under the meat on the cooler side of the barbecue.

Rub off as much of the marinade as you can and retain it. Place the meat on the grill and cook until it reaches an internal temperature of 51°C (125°F) – make sure you place your meat thermometer into the thickest part of the leg. Mine took 30 minutes to reach that heat but remember, cook to temperature, not time. It's ready when it's ready.

Transfer the meat to a plate and baste it with a little melted ghee. Then build up your fire for direct heat cooking. I usually cover the barbecue and open the vents to bring it up to around 370°C (700°F).

Once you have a good searing heat, place the meat over the direct heat on the grill and sear for 1–2 minutes on each side. Transfer to a serving platter and cover with foil to rest for a good 15 minutes.

When ready to serve, slice the meat thinly across the grain. Drizzle with any remaining ghee and sprinkle with sea salt. I like to serve this with green chutney (made with mint leaves) or else heat up the remaining marinade until simmering and drizzle that over the meat.

HANGING SMOKED LEG OF LAMB
SERVES 6-8

This recipe relies only on the quality of the lamb used and the delicious smoky flavour it gets from cooking long and slow over the fire. It's another take on the lamb namak mandi on page 44 but with a larger chunk of meat. This hanging smoked lamb roast is made for lazy days, sitting by the fire with friends while enjoying a few drinks and snacks, eagerly awaiting a perfectly cooked lamb dinner. For this cooking method you need to build a campfire either on the ground or in a Kadai fire bowl/BBQ. You will also need a way of hanging the meat over the fire. Buy a tripod hanger with a hook or use a tree branch and some wire. Both will work.

PREP TIME: 10 MINS
COOKING TIME: 4-5 HOURS

250ml (1 cup) cider vinegar
3 tbsp garlic and ginger paste
    (see page 169)
4 generous tbsp sea salt
1 leg of lamb (approx.
    2–2.5kg/4½–5½lb)

TO SERVE
Chapatis or naans
Salad
Green chutney (see page 162)

Pour 500ml (2 cups) water into a spray bottle with the vinegar and add the garlic and ginger paste and salt. Shake it until the salt dissolves into the water.

Now build a good-sized fire (see page 10) with a little flame and lots of smoke and hang the meat, securing it through the bone near the ankle with a butcher's hook or strong wire. The meat needs to hang 30–60cm (1–2ft) from the flame while cooking. This is a lengthy cooking process and you will need to adjust the height of the lamb leg from time to time or spread the wood to the sides.

Cook for 4–5 hours, squirting the leg with the water mixture every half hour or so. As the meat cooks, it will take on the smokiness from the fire. It smells amazing and believe me... the flavour is worth waiting for.

When the lamb reaches an internal temperature of 60°C (140°F) it will be cooked to a delicious medium rare.

Transfer to a cutting board and slice – there's no need to leave it to rest as it has been resting the whole time it was cooking. Serve with chapatis or naans, salad and green chutney.

NOTE
Depending on the size of your leg of lamb, you might find that the shank is not cooking through as quickly as the top of the leg hanging closest to the fire. No problem! Just unhook the meat and throw the whole thing directly onto the hot coals. Move it around from time to time, ensuring the rarest part is on the highest heat and cook to your preferred doneness.

I've also made this with a huge leg of lamb, about 4kg (9lb) total weight, which took about 6 hours to cook. So this method works with any size, as long as you cook to temperature, not to time!

SWEET AND SPICY BABY BACK RIBS
SERVES 4–6

There was no way I could write a barbecue cookbook without sharing my spicy baby back ribs recipe with you. Over the years it has become a recipe I have to make at least twice every summer and sometimes even in the cold of winter. Low and slow is the rule here! These are not sticky ribs. If that is what you prefer, try my all-purpose rub (see page 168) and then add some of my all-purpose BBQ sauce (see page 166) for the last 30 minutes of cooking. This recipe relies solely on the natural juiciness of the pork ribs and they're so good with a cold beer.

PREP TIME: 10 MINS
COOKING TIME: 4 HOURS

4 racks of meaty baby back
   pork ribs

FOR THE SPICE RUB
2 tbsp garlic powder
2 tbsp onion powder
2 tbsp ground black pepper
2 tbsp salt
100g (3½oz) light brown sugar
1–2 tbsp Kashmiri chilli powder
4 tbsp paprika
1 tbsp ground cumin
1 tbsp ground coriander

FOR THE VINEGAR SPRAY
250ml (1 cup) cider vinegar
1 tbsp Worcestershire sauce
Juice of 2 limes
2 squirts of Tabasco (more or
   less to taste)
Salt and freshly ground black
   pepper, to taste

Stir together all of the spice rub ingredients. Dry the ribs with a paper towel and then cover them with the dry rub. No binder such as oil is required. Once you've covered the ribs with the rub, give them a shake. Whatever rub falls off shouldn't be there. If the ribs have too much rub on them, they won't get the smoky flavour that makes them so good.

Set up your barbecue for indirect heat cooking (see page 9) and adjust the temperature so that it is maintaining a steady 125°C (257°F). You can adjust the temperature by opening or closing the top and bottom vents (see page 10). If the temperature falls below 107°C (225°F), add a few more burning briquettes. You will need to do this from time to time as this is a long cook.

Place a drip tray with a little water in it under the cooking grate, opposite the burning coals. This isn't necessary if using a ceramic barbecue. Then place the ribs on the grate on the cooler side of the barbecue. If space is an issue, you could stand them on their side. Close the lid and cook for about 2 hours, watching the temperature carefully. Meanwhile, prepare the vinegar spray by mixing everything together in a spray bottle.

After 2 hours, the ribs will begin to look a bit dry. Spray them with a little of the vinegar spray. Continue to do this every 30 minutes, or whenever the ribs are looking a bit thirsty. Cook for a further 2 hours. After 4 hours of cooking, the ribs should be ready, but remember, this is barbecue. The ribs are ready when they're ready! To check for doneness, try pulling them apart. If they come apart easily, they're ready to serve.

Although these juicy and smoky ribs are delicious on their own, I like to serve them with a little of my all-purpose BBQ sauce (see page 166) for dipping.

GERMAN CURRYWURST
SERVES 4

You might have experienced or even cooked sausages on your barbecue that were blackened on the exterior but still quite raw in the centre. Try the method for cooking sausages below and that will never happen to you again.

I was first introduced to currywurst back in 1986 while studying in Tübingen, Germany. While walking back from class every day, my friends and I would always stop by a fast food *imbiss* for beer and food. Currywurst was a cheap snack we ordered all the time. We weren't alone; around 800,000,000 portions of currywurst are consumed in Germany every year. The most accepted version of its origins is that in post-World War II Berlin a couple of British soldiers traded curry powder and ketchup with a woman named Herta Heuwer for some spirits. She used her new ingredients to come up with currywurst and the rest is history. Currywurst is normally served in a bread roll with lots of sauce drizzled over it; I like to cut the sausages up and serve them in the sauce. Both options are delicious.

PREP TIME: 10 MINS
COOKING TIME: 40 MINS

2 tbsp rapeseed (canola) oil
1 onion, very finely chopped
1 garlic clove, minced
2 green bird's eye chillies
2 tsp Kashmiri chilli powder
   (more or less to taste)
½ tsp ground coriander
½ tsp ground cumin
1 tbsp curry powder, plus extra
   to garnish
400g (14oz) tinned (canned)
   chopped tomatoes
250ml (1 cup) ketchup
1 tbsp concentrated tomato paste
1 tsp German mustard or Dijon
1 tbsp Worcestershire sauce
6 German bratwurst or
   bockwurst, or another
   European sausage
Salt, to taste
Masala garlic fries (see page 146)
   or rolls, to serve

Prepare a direct heat fire (see page 10). When hot, place a large saucepan or wok over a high heat and another saucepan filled with water next to it. Cover the pan with water in it and bring to a boil while you are preparing the sauce.

Add the oil to the empty wok or saucepan and when visibly hot, stir in the chopped onion. Fry for about 5 minutes, or until soft and translucent. Stir in the garlic and whole chillies and fry for a further 30 seconds.

Next add the ground spices and stir them into the onion mixture. Add the tinned (canned) tomatoes, ketchup and tomato paste and stir to combine. Add about 250ml (1 cup) water and bring to a simmer and then stir in the mustard and Worcestershire sauce. Season to taste.

Continue simmering the sauce to thicken slightly. Classic currywurst sauce is quite smooth, so you could blend this sauce if you like or just let it break down as it simmers. Keep warm.

Once the water is boiling, drop in the sausages and simmer for about 15 minutes, or until cooked through. Bratwurst is usually sold raw but bockwurst is cooked, like a hotdog, so no need to check if using those. Transfer to a plate.

To finish, grill the sausages on the cooking grate of your barbecue over a medium-high heat until browned all over. You can serve these the traditional way, on a bread roll and smothered with the sauce, or cut them up, add them to the sauce and serve as you would a curry.

Left: German currywurst
Right: Masala garlic fries (page 146)

PULLED PORK BUTT
SERVES 10–12

You will need to start this recipe early! The day I cooked my first Boston pork butt was the day I truly fell in love with barbecue. It was the late 1980s and I was quite a barbecue novice at the time. With the help of a few tips from a chef friend I was able to cook it to perfection, but it took a long time. When I'm spending the day outdoors, I make this on my Kamado Joe, cooking it low and slow for 7–8 hours. This is the perfect cut to cook on a pellet barbecue, though, as you can set the temperature and then pretty much forget about it. Other than maintaining that important cooking temperature, this recipe is so simple. You will need foil for wrapping the pork while cooking.

PREP TIME: 10 MINS
COOKING TIME:
7–9 HOURS, PLUS
RESTING TIME

3kg (7lb) bone-in Boston pork butt
6 tbsp all-purpose rub (see page 169)
125ml (½ cup) cider vinegar
500ml (2 cups) my all-purpose BBQ sauce (see page 166), plus extra to serve
Breads and garnishes, to serve (optional)

Rub the meat all over with 4 tablespoons of the all-purpose rub. This is best done a day in advance but even a couple of hours before cooking is fine if more convenient. Build an indirect heat fire (see page 9). Once the coals have ashed over and are really hot, shift them all over to one side of the barbecue and place a drip pan, half-filled with water, on the side with no coals. If using a ceramic barbecue there is no need to use a drip pan.

Close the lid and ensure the top and bottom vents are fully open. After about 30 minutes, you can start adjusting the heat. For low and slow cooking like this, limit the air flow into the barbecue by semi-closing the bottom vent. Leave the top vent open and then start adjusting the heat by closing the top vent a little until you have a steady 110°C (225°F) cooking temperature. Do all the fine-tuning using the top vent, opening it wider to increase the temperature or closing it a little if too hot. Be sure to check the temperature every 45 minutes and add a few more lit briquettes to the burning charcoal if the barbecue is not maintaining that heat.

Once you've got the heat right, place the prepared pork, skin side down, on the grill on the cool side of the barbecue and close the lid. In a spray bottle, combine the vinegar with the remaining all-purpose rub and spray the meat from time to time when it's looking thirsty.

After about 4 hours of cooking at 110°C (225°F), the pork will have taken in a good amount of tasty smoke flavour and will be a beautiful deep brown colour. Transfer it to a clean surface, wrap it tightly in a few layers of foil and then place it back on the grill to continue cooking for another 3–5 hours. To check for doneness, push the meat with your finger. If it doesn't spring back at you, it will be ready for pulling.

Remove from the heat and leave to rest for 1–2 hours in the foil wrap. Once rested, shred the meat and stir in the barbecue sauce. If pulling by hand, it will still be very hot so use gloves. Serve on its own with more barbecue sauce as a dip or pile it high on a bun or naan with the garnishes of your choice. You'll see from the photograph opposite that I also like it with a green chutney (see page 162) too!

TANDOORI SALMON
WITH CABBAGE STIR FRY
SERVES 4

This is my play on an outstanding salmon and cabbage recipe sent to me by my friend, chef Jomon Kuriakose, who is chef de cuisine at The LaLiT London. I decided to try it on the barbecue, which gave the salmon a delicious smoky flavour, but you could also sear the salmon in a hot, lightly oiled pan for 3–4 minutes on each side, as per Jomon's original recipe. I've given instructions for cooking the sauce and cabbage inside, on the hob, but you could also cook these on the barbecue, if you have already fired it up to cook the salmon.

PREP TIME: 10 MINS. PLUS
MARINATING TIME
COOKING TIME: 20 MINS

½ tsp salt, plus extra to taste
½ tsp freshly ground black
  pepper
2 tsp garlic and ginger paste (see
  page 169)
4 x 125g (4½oz) salmon fillets,
  skin on
Rapeseed (canola) oil, for
  brushing

FOR THE SAUCE

2 generous tbsp ghee
20 fresh or frozen curry leaves
1 onion, finely chopped
3 garlic cloves, finely chopped
1–2 tsp dried red chilli flakes
  (more or less to taste)
½ tsp ground turmeric
1 tsp ground coriander
4 cherry tomatoes, halved
250ml (1 cup) thick coconut milk

FOR THE CABBAGE STIR FRY

2 tbsp rapeseed (canola) or
  coconut oil
1 tsp black mustard seeds
20 fresh or frozen curry leaves
300g (10½oz) red cabbage,
  thinly sliced
50g (2oz) fresh or frozen grated
  coconut
Lemon juice, to taste

Rub the salt, pepper and garlic and ginger paste into the salmon fillets, getting it right into the flesh. Cover and leave to marinate in the fridge for 30 minutes, or up to 2 hours. Meanwhile, prepare the sauce. Place a saucepan over a medium-high heat and add the ghee. When it starts to sizzle, stir in the curry leaves and fry for about 20 seconds to flavour the ghee. Stir in the chopped onion and fry for about 5 minutes, or until golden brown, then stir in the chopped garlic and chilli flakes. Fry for about a minute and then stir in the ground spices, tomatoes and coconut milk and simmer for about 5 minutes to thicken slightly. Keep warm.

To make the cabbage stir fry, heat the oil in a frying pan over a high heat. When visibly hot, stir in the black mustard seeds. When they begin to crackle, stir in the curry leaves and fry for 30 seconds. Add the cabbage and grated coconut and fry until the cabbage is soft but still has a bit of bite to it. Season with salt and a little lemon juice. Remove from the heat and keep warm.

To cook the salmon, heat up your barbecue grate as hot as you can get it. Dry any moisture from the surface of the fish with a paper towel and brush the fish and the cooking grate lightly with oil.

Place the salmon on the cooking grate skin side up and close the lid. Cook for 3 minutes and then lift the lid. The fish should come off easily. If it doesn't, gently pry it off with a metal spatula but don't force it. The fish will easily come off the grill when it is ready. Flip the fish over and cook for 3–5 minutes, or until the skin is crispy but the fish is still a bit pink in the centre. At this stage you could also sear the sides to make grill marks but be careful not to overcook the fish. Transfer the salmon steaks to a warm serving platter and keep warm. This is a good time to reheat your cabbage and sauce, if necessary, by placing it back on the hot cooking grate.

To serve, spoon some of the sauce onto one side of a plate and place the seared salmon on top, then place some of the stir-fried cabbage next to it.

CEDAR PLANK SALMON WITH CHILLI, GARLIC AND LEMON OIL
SERVES 4

Cooking salmon on soaked cedar planks is easy and always goes down well. You could of course purchase some chilli-garlic oil but from my experience, the shop-bought stuff rarely comes close to the amazing flavour you get when you make your own. The lemon and garlic flavours in the chilli oil go so well with the salmon.

PREP TIME: 15 MINS, PLUS SOAKING TIME
COOKING TIME: 15 MINS

1 side of salmon, skin on
4 tsp all-purpose rub (see page 169)
2 lemons, sliced
3 tbsp finely chopped coriander (cilantro)

FOR THE CHILLI, GARLIC AND LEMON OIL

750ml (3 cups) rapeseed (canola) oil
85g (3oz) good-quality dried red chilli flakes
100g (3½oz) garlic cloves, finely chopped
2 lemongrass stalks, pounded and cut into paper-thin slices
5 spring onions (scallions), sliced
Zest of 3 lemons
1 tsp salt

Soak the cedar plank in water for at least 30 minutes.

Meanwhile, make the chilli-garlic oil. Put all the oil ingredients in a saucepan and bring to a steady simmer over a medium heat. It is important to simmer the oil at around 110°C (225°F) and no hotter than 120°C (245°F). Use a thermometer and watch it closely to ensure the ingredients don't burn. Simmer for 15 minutes then allow to cool a little. Pour into a clean glass jar and store at room temperature in a cool, dry place.

Set up your barbecue for indirect heat cooking (see page 9). Close the lid and bring to 150°C (300°F). When ready to cook, place the soaked cedar plank over the cooler side, close the lid and leave for 2 minutes.

Sprinkle the salmon with the all-purpose rub and cover with the lemon slices. Place the salmon on the plank, cover and cook for 15 minutes, which will keep the fish a bit pink in the centre, or longer if you like it more well done. Serve, garnished with the coriander (cilantro) and some of the chilli, garlic and lemon oil. I also like to top it with some of the garlic and citrus-flavoured goop at the bottom.

HARIYALI HALIBUT SKEWERS
SERVES 4

I use this hariyali fish marinade for many different recipes, as it's equally as good smothered over chicken, lamb or prawns (shrimp). If using it as a meat marinade, I add a couple more tablespoons of yoghurt and let it marinate for at least 6 hours, or overnight. Fish only needs to marinate for about 20 minutes, or less if time is an issue. I use halibut in this recipe but you could use any meaty fish such as cod, monkfish or salmon.

I cooked this in my tandoor oven – if you are one of the growing number of people who have one too, see https://greatcurryrecipes.net/how-to-use-a-tandoor-oven/ for instructions on cooking in a tandoor.

PREP TIME: 15 MINS, PLUS MARINATING TIME
COOKING TIME: 10 MINS

600g (1lb 5oz) halibut or another meaty fish, cut into chunks
½ tsp ground turmeric
1½ tbsp garlic and ginger paste (see page 169)
½ tsp rapeseed (canola) oil, plus extra for greasing
½ tsp salt
½ tsp ground black pepper
2 tbsp lime or lemon juice
Flaky sea salt, to serve
Chapatis and green salad, to serve

FOR THE HARIYALI MARINADE

30g (1 packed cup) coriander (cilantro)
20g (¾ cup) mint leaves
10 fresh or frozen curry leaves
6 green bird's eye chillies, roughly chopped (more or less to taste)
½ red onion, roughly chopped
1 tbsp ground cumin
1 tsp ground coriander
1 tsp amchoor (dried mango powder)
2 tbsp Greek yoghurt

Put the fish into a large bowl and add the turmeric, garlic and ginger paste, oil, salt, pepper and lime or lemon juice. Mix well, then set aside while you make the hariyali marinade.

Put the coriander (cilantro), mint leaves, curry leaves, chillies, onion, ground cumin, coriander and amchoor (dried mango powder) into a blender and blend with just enough water to make a thick but smooth paste. The marinade should not be at all watery so be careful when adding the water. Scrape the paste into a bowl and mix in the yoghurt, then pour the marinade all over the fish, rubbing it in well. Cover and leave to marinate for up to 20 minutes.

Prepare a direct heat fire (see page 10). When the coals are white-hot and it is uncomfortable to hold your hand at cooking height for more than 2 seconds, you're ready to cook.

Lightly grease your skewers with oil and then weave the fish onto the skewers. Don't just stick the skewer straight through or the fish will be difficult to rotate and won't cook evenly.

Lay the skewers above the fire and cook until the fish begins to char on the underside, then rotate the skewers to cook the other side. Continue rotating until the fish is cooked through – this should only take about 10 minutes but watch it closely so that you don't overcook the fish. Season with flaky sea salt and serve with chapatis and perhaps a good green salad.

Red: Grilled tandoori octopus (page 82)
Green: Hariyali halibut skewers

GRILLED TANDOORI OCTOPUS
SERVES 2–4

I have always loved octopus. Back in my younger years, my family cooked Italian-style grilled octopus at least once a year. It was a lot more difficult to find back then. Octopus can be tough if not cooked properly, but follow the instructions below and it will be deliciously tender every time.

PREP TIME: 20 MINS
COOKING TIME: 1 HOUR
45 MINS

450g (1lb) octopus, cleaned and
    with eyes and beak removed
    (ask your fishmonger to do
    this for you)
Lemon wedges, to serve
Coriander chutney or raita,
    to serve

FOR THE COOKING LIQUID
1 tbsp Kashmiri chilli powder
1 tbsp ground turmeric
2 tbsp garlic and ginger paste
    (see page 169)
1 tsp black peppercorns
1 Indian bay leaf
1 tbsp tandoori masala
    (see page 167)

FOR THE MARINADE
4 generous tbsp Greek yoghurt
2 tbsp mustard oil
2 tbsp garlic and ginger paste
    (see page 169)
1 tbsp Kashmiri chilli powder
1 tbsp tandoori masala
    (see page 167)
1 tsp ground turmeric
2 tsp ground coriander
½ tsp salt, plus extra to taste
2 tsp finely chopped green
    chillies
Juice of 1 lemon

If cleaning the octopus yourself, place it on a clean work surface. Slice off the small head with the eyes on it. Just cut behind those eyes and slice it all off. Flip the octopus over and you will see a black spot right in the centre of all the tentacles. That's the beak. Carefully carve it out with a sharp knife.

Pound the octopus all over with a meat mallet. This will make the octopus really tender. Set aside.

Bring a large pot of water to a boil and add the cooking liquid ingredients. Place the octopus in the water, lower the heat to medium and simmer for 1½ hours.

While the octopus is simmering, stir together or blend all the marinade ingredients and set aside.

After 1½ hours, transfer the octopus to a cutting board and cut into bite-size pieces. Put the pieces into a bowl with the marinade and leave to marinate for 30 minutes.

Prepare a direct heat fire (see page 10). When the coals are white-hot and it is uncomfortable to hold your hand at cooking height for more than 2 seconds, you're ready to cook. Skewer the octopus pieces and place over the coals. Grill until the octopus is nicely browned and charred in some places. Be sure to turn often so that the meat cooks and chars evenly. Season with more salt if you like and serve with lemon wedges, coriander chutney and/or a good raita.

COCONUT AND MANGO JUMBO PRAWNS

SERVES 4

What a combo! Coconut and mango go so well with prawns (shrimp). The marinade is also used as a dipping sauce, which can be served hot or cold. I like to use jumbo prawns with the head and shells still on. They are grilled over intense heat to blacken and then eaten with your hands at the table with the sauce. Yes, it's a bit messy, but the best meals often are!

PREP TIME: 10 MINS, PLUS MARINATING TIME
COOKING TIME: 10 MINS

8 jumbo prawns (shrimp), deveined

FOR THE MARINADE
1 mango, roughly chopped
2 tomatoes, roughly chopped
3 green bird's eye chillies, roughly chopped
5 small shallots, roughly chopped
20 fresh or frozen curry leaves
2 tbsp garlic and ginger paste (see page 169)
1 tbsp melted coconut oil, plus extra for basting
1 tsp freshly ground black pepper
Flaky sea salt, to taste

Put all the marinade ingredients into a blender or food processor and blend to a smooth paste. Transfer half of the paste to a mixing bowl and add the prawns (shrimp). Mix well – as you are cooking these with the shell on, it is important to get underneath the shell with your fingers to rub the marinade right into the flesh. Marinate for about 20 minutes.

Prepare a direct heat fire (see page 10). When the coals are white-hot and it is uncomfortable to hold your hand 5cm (2in) above the grill for more than 2 seconds, you're ready to cook.

Lightly brush the grill with coconut oil and place the prawns on the grill. Cook for about 3 minutes, or until the underside is beginning to char, then flip them over to cook the other side. Baste from time to time with coconut oil. Grill until nicely charred and cooked through. Meanwhile, if serving the sauce warm, gently heat the remaining marinade. Otherwise serve it at room temperature. Season the prawns with flaky sea salt before serving.

TANDOORI GRILLED CALAMARI WITH FRESH MANGO CHUTNEY
SERVES 6

This is most definitely beach grub! When I light up a grill by the sea, I like to cook seafood and lots of it. This grilled calamari recipe is really easy to whip up and can be enjoyed right off the skewer. I suggest getting a few plates, though, as the mango chutney with its savoury, sweet, spicy and sour flavours is the perfect accompaniment. Soaking the squid in milk overnight makes it really tender. Make this charred squid, pop open some wine and enjoy.

PREP TIME: 15 MINS, PLUS MARINATING TIME
COOKING TIME: 12 MINS

1kg (2lb 4oz) baby squid, cleaned and soaked in milk overnight
125ml (½ cup) extra virgin olive oil
3 spring onions (scallions), thinly sliced
1 tbsp garlic and ginger paste (see page 169)
1 tbsp tandoori masala (see page 167)
1 tsp dried red chilli flakes
2 tbsp finely chopped coriander (cilantro)
5 lemons, thinly sliced
30 fresh lime leaves (or bay leaves)
Salt and freshly ground black pepper, to taste

FOR THE FRESH MANGO CHUTNEY
1 mango, finely diced
1 red (bell) pepper, finely chopped
½ red onion, finely diced
1 garlic clove, minced
2 green bird's eye chillies, finely chopped (more or less to taste)
1 tbsp finely chopped coriander (cilantro)
Juice of 1 lime

Rinse the milk off the squid and slice the bodies in half widthways. Put the bodies and tentacles into a mixing bowl and add the oil, spring onions (scallions), garlic and ginger paste, tandoori masala, chilli flakes, coriander (cilantro) and salt and pepper to taste. Mix well to coat. Cover and leave to marinate in the fridge for 30–60 minutes.

Now prepare the fresh mango chutney. Put all the ingredients into a bowl, season and stir well to combine. Taste and adjust by adding more chillies, salt or pepper.

When ready to cook, prepare a direct heat fire (see page 10). When the coals are white-hot and it is uncomfortable to hold your hand at cooking height for more than 2 seconds, you're ready to cook.

Thread the squid, lemon slices and lime leaves onto skewers, alternating so that each piece of squid gets a bit of lemon and lime flavour. Reserve any leftover marinade. Grill the skewers over a high heat for 6 minutes on one side, then rotate to cook the other side until the squid is completely cooked through and nicely charred. This should take a further 5–6 minutes. Be sure to baste with the reserved marinade from time to time. Serve hot with the fresh mango chutney.

Left: Tandoori grilled calamari
Right: Homemade papads (page 13)

GRILLED MONKFISH SKEWERS
SERVES 6

Monkfish is amazing cooked over the coals. The marinade for this recipe will work with any fish, meat or vegetables. If you have a good fishmonger, ask them to prepare the monkfish for you by removing the thin membrane from the meat. You could do this yourself but I find fishmongers do it a lot faster!

PREP TIME: 15 MINS
COOKING TIME: 15 MINS

1 whole monkfish tail (about 800g/1lb 12oz), bone and thin membrane removed and cut into chunks
1 red (bell) pepper, cut into similar-size pieces
1 green (bell) pepper, cut into similar-size pieces
1 large red onion, cut into similar-size pieces
Flaky sea salt, to taste
Lemon wedges, to serve

FOR THE MARINADE
2 tsp gram (chickpea) flour
Juice of 1 lemon
½ tsp salt
2 tbsp garlic, ginger and chilli paste (see page 169)
1 tsp ground cumin
2 tbsp Greek yoghurt
1 tsp Kashmiri chilli powder
1 tsp garam masala (see page 168) or tandoori masala (see page 167)
2 tbsp finely chopped coriander (cilantro)

Start with the marinade. Place a dry frying pan over a medium heat and toast the gram (chickpea) flour for a couple of minutes, stirring continuously until fragrant and a couple of shades darker. Tip into a bowl and allow to cool, then add all the remaining marinade ingredients and whisk until smooth.

Add the monkfish and vegetables and mix well so that the monkfish is coated all over with the marinade. Set aside while you prepare a direct heat fire (see page 10).

When the coals are white-hot and it is uncomfortable to hold your hand 5cm (2in) above cooking height for more than 2 seconds, you're ready to cook. Skewer the monkfish and vegetables and place over the coals. Cook for 10–15 minutes, rotating from time to time, until cooked through and nicely charred in places.

Sprinkle with flaky sea salt and serve hot with lemon wedges.

AGED MANGO PANEER SKEWERS
SERVES 4

Anyone who has read my previous books will know that I love to try new recipes from chefs who are cooking up awesome food. This recipe was sent to me by my friends at Pataka in London. I like to serve the grilled paneer on hot chapatis. The amount of mango pickle used in this recipe is quite small but it adds so much to the flavour so do try to find it if you can. It's available at Asian markets and online. This marinated paneer is also delicious stirred into a curry, as I did on page 140.

PREP TIME: 20 MINS, PLUS MARINATING TIME
COOKING TIME: 10 MINS

600g (1lb 5oz) paneer cheese, cut into 5cm (2in) cubes and pricked with a fork
1 red (bell) pepper, cut into 5cm (2in) pieces
1 green (bell) pepper, cut into 5cm (2in) pieces
1 red onion, cut into 5cm (2in) pieces

FOR THE SPICE BLEND
1 tsp black mustard seeds
1 tsp cumin seeds
1 tsp fennel seeds
1 tsp onion seeds
1 tsp ajwain (carom) seeds
¼ tsp fenugreek seeds
2 dried Kashmiri chillies

FOR THE MARINADE
2 tbsp gram (chickpea) flour
75ml (¼ cup) rapeseed (canola) oil
1 tsp ground turmeric
350g (1½ cups) Greek yoghurt
1 tsp Kashmiri chilli powder (more or less to taste)
2 tsp garam masala (see page 168)
Juice of 1 lemon
¼ tsp ground fenugreek
1 tsp mango pickle (or more to taste), very finely chopped

First prepare the spice blend. Dry roast the whole spices in a dry frying pan over a medium heat until warm to the touch and fragrant but not yet smoking. This should only take about 3 minutes. Transfer to a plate to cool, then grind into a coarse powder.

Next make the marinade. Place a dry frying pan over a medium heat and add the gram (chickpea) flour. Stir for a couple of minutes until fragrant and a couple of shades darker. Set aside to cool. Heat the oil in a small saucepan over a medium heat until hot but not boiling, then stir in the ground turmeric. In a bowl, whisk together the remaining marinade ingredients, including the toasted gram flour, then add the turmeric oil and 1 tablespoon of the spice blend. Test and add more to taste – I use it all. Whisk until smooth and then add the cubed paneer and vegetables. Cover and leave to marinate for at least 1 hour, or overnight if you have time.

When ready to cook, prepare a direct heat fire (see page 10). Skewer the paneer and vegetables and place over the hottest part of the fire. Be sure to turn them regularly, basting with the remaining marinade. Cook for about 10 minutes, or until the paneer is soft, golden and charred in places. Move the skewers to a cooler part of the barbecue if they char too quickly.

GRILLED SWEET POTATOES WITH AVOCADO CHUTNEY

SERVES 4

Vegetarian food in India is always delicious, sometimes exciting and never boring. This is a filling and healthy main dish made with grilled sweet potatoes, which is also delicious as a starter. The avocado chutney is the perfect accompaniment for this quick and easy dish.

PREP TIME: 10 MINS
COOKING TIME: 15 MINS

4 sweet potatoes, peeled and sliced into 12 x 1.25cm (½in) rounds
1 tbsp coconut oil, plus extra for brushing
6 shallots, roughly chopped
1 tsp Kashmiri chilli powder
½ tsp ground turmeric
1 tsp tamarind paste
1 generous tbsp finely chopped ginger
10 fresh or frozen curry leaves
2 tbsp melted butter or ghee
Salt to, taste

FOR THE AVOCADO CHUTNEY

1 avocado, diced
4 shallots, finely chopped
3 green bird's eye chillies, finely chopped
1 tomato, deseeded and diced
Juice of ½ lemon
Flaky sea salt, to taste

First make the avocado chutney. Put all the ingredients into a small bowl, season with salt and stir to combine. Cover and put in the fridge until ready to serve.

Bring a large saucepan of water to a boil and parboil the sweet potato slices for about 5 minutes, until about 90% cooked. There should still be a bit of resistance when pricked with a fork. Drain the sweet potatoes and transfer to a plate to cool.

Put the coconut oil, shallots, chilli powder, turmeric, tamarind paste, ginger and curry leaves into a blender or food processor and blend to a thick paste. Season to taste with salt.

Once the sweet potatoes have cooled, cover them completely with the marinade paste and set to one side while you fire up the grill. When the coals are white-hot and it is uncomfortable to hold your hand 5cm (2in) above the grill for more than 2 seconds, you're ready to cook.

Lightly brush the grill with oil and then place the sweet potatoes on the grill. Cook for about 4 minutes, or until dark grill marks appear on the underside of the sweet potatoes, and then flip them over to grill the other side. Brush each slice with melted butter or ghee and season with salt to taste. To serve, place the grilled sweet potatoes onto plates and top with the avocado chutney.

INDIAN CHILLI-LIME STREET CORN ON THE COB

SERVES 6

Corn on the cob is perfect for cooking either on the grate or in the embers of a fire. Corn cooked in this way originates from Mexico but it is really popular in India, too. I included a different version of this recipe in my book *The Curry Guy Veggie*, but this is how I make it now. It simply wouldn't be right to leave this recipe out of the book!

PREP TIME: 5 MINS
COOKING TIME: 10 MINS

2 tbsp ground cumin
1 tbsp Kashmiri chilli powder (more or less to taste)
1 tbsp chaat masala or garam masala (see page 168)
125ml (½ cup) melted ghee or butter
4 garlic cloves, very finely chopped
6 corn on the cobs (ears of corn)
2 limes, quartered
Flaky sea salt, to taste

Mix together the ground spices with some salt on a plate and set aside.

Prepare a direct heat fire (see page 10). When the coals are white-hot and it is uncomfortable to hold your hand 5cm (2in) above the grill for more than 2 seconds, place the ghee or butter and chopped garlic in a small saucepan and heat it over the fire. Keep a watchful eye on it so that you don't burn the garlic. Now place the ears of corn either on the cooking grate or directly in the coals. As the corn cooks, it will begin to crackle. Move it around with tongs so that it cooks evenly. It will blacken in some areas, which adds to the flavour and presentation.

Once the corn has cooked to your liking, brush it with the garlic and ghee/butter mixture, or if you have a large plate or dish you could roll it in the mixture. When well coated, roll the ears of corn in the ground spices and salt. Season with a little more flaky salt if you like. Serve with the lime wedges to squeeze over the corn before every delicious bite.

PAN-COOKED MAINS

Most things that can be cooked indoors can also be cooked outdoors, and often with even better results. For me, there's just something that little bit better about a curry or biryani cooked over fire. Making homemade naans or rotis in a tandoor or a pan gets fantastic results too and I think you'll love bringing all this delicious outdoor cooking to the table just as much as I do.

As well as kebabs, burgers and pan-fried dishes, in this section I have included some great curries for you to try – but don't limit yourself just to them. Any curry can be cooked over fire, bringing with it a more rustic and even more traditional flavour. So, if you have one or more of my other cookbooks, give some recipes from them a try outdoors too.

MINCED DONER KEBABS
SERVES 10

The original doner kebab might be Turkish in origin, but it has also become very popular at many Indian takeaways – as my recipe for Sylheti shatkora doner on page 94 demonstrates. Traditionally, huge upright spits of minced (ground) meat are cooked rotisserie style, with the meat shaved off as it becomes crisp. I tried recreating this on a small upright rotisserie, but it just wasn't the same as a professional doner kebab rotisserie. I promise, however, that with the method below, you will get fantastic, takeaway-quality results. I prefer to make this in large batches and freeze the leftovers, but feel free to halve this recipe.

PREP TIME: 25 MINS, PLUS COOLING TIME
COOKING TIME: 2 HOURS 15 MINS

2 onions, roughly chopped
2kg (4½lb) 20% fat minced (ground) beef or lamb
3 tbsp Greek yoghurt
1 tbsp salt
1½ tsp ground black pepper
2 tsp garlic powder
1 tbsp paprika or chilli powder
1 tbsp thyme leaves
1 tbsp dried oregano
3 tbsp rapeseed (canola) oil (optional)

FOR THE SALAD
2 red onions, thinly sliced
1 carrot, grated
½ red or white cabbage, thinly sliced
1 head of cos or iceberg lettuce, thinly sliced
Juice of 1 lemon
Salt, to taste

TO SERVE
Naans or chapatis
Kebab-shop garlic sauce (see page 165)
Kebab-shop red chilli sauce (see page 165)

Grate the onions, transfer to a muslin (cheesecloth) and twist into a ball as tightly as you can to extract the onion juice into a bowl. (The remaining onions can be used for the beef chapli kebab burger recipe on page 126.) Pour the onion juice into a food processor and add the remaining kebab ingredients, apart from the oil. Blend to a fine paste. It is important that the meat is finely blended, so you may need to do this in batches. Form the mixture into two meat loaves and place each one in an ovenproof roasting pan. Cover loosely with foil.

Set up your barbecue for indirect heat cooking (see page 9). You will need to cook the meat at between 180°C (355°F) and 200°C (400°F) for 2 hours. This step can of course be done in an oven if you prefer, but I love the smoky flavour you get from cooking on the barbecue. After 2 hours, the meat loaves will be cooked and there will be a lot of meat juices in the pans. Retain the meat juices for later and place the cooked meat loaves in the fridge to cool and harden. You could speed this process up by placing them in the freezer once cooled a little. Once cold, take a sharp chef's knife and slice the meat into thin strips.

To finish, prepare a direct heat fire (see page 10). Place a frying pan on the grate over the hottest part of the fire and add the rapeseed (canola) oil, or leftover fat from the roasting pans. Once hot, cook the meat slices in batches until crispy. Pour in a little of the reserved cooking juices to moisten up the meat, then transfer to a bowl and keep warm. Repeat with the remaining meat slices, adding more oil/fat as required.

Make the salad by mixing together the onions, carrot, cabbage and lettuce in a large bowl and dressing with the lemon juice and salt. Serve the doner meat on naans or chapatis with the salad and sauces.

NOTE
I recommend frying a small amount of the meat to check for seasoning, before forming it into loaves to cook.

SYLHETI SHATKORA DONER
SERVES 4-6

This is a popular Bangladeshi way to serve doner meat that is just as popular in the UK as it is in the subcontinent. If the thought of making your own doner meat doesn't appeal, you can find prepared doner meat in the frozen section at many Asian grocers. Homemade is so much better, though, so I recommend making some. You can use half the quantity to make traditional doner kebabs and the other half to make this spicier version. Frozen shatkora is available at most Asian grocers but you could also substitute a tablespoon or so of shatkora pickle. You could also substitute lime pickle, but it's not quite the same.

PREP TIME: 15 MINS
COOKING TIME: 20-25 MINS

4 tbsp rapeseed (canola) oil
½ batch minced doner kebab meat (see page 92), cooked and sliced
1 onion, finely chopped
2 tbsp garlic and ginger paste (see page 169)
1 tsp Kashmiri chilli powder
1 tbsp ground cumin
1 tsp ground coriander
½ tsp ground turmeric
1 tbsp garam masala (see page 168)
250ml (1 cup) low-salt beef stock or water
Rind from 2 shatkora wedges (about ½ whole fruit), cut into 3 pieces
2 tsp naga pickle (I use Mr Naga brand)
1 tomato, quartered
Large handful of coriander (cilantro), roughly chopped
Salt, to taste

TO SERVE
Naans or rotis
Salad
Kebab-shop garlic sauce (see page 165)
Kebab-shop red chilli sauce (see page 165)

Heat 2 tablespoons of the oil in a frying pan or karahi over a high heat. When visibly hot, stir in the sliced doner meat and fry, stirring from time to time, until crispy in places; this should take 5–10 minutes. Transfer to a plate.

Add the remaining oil to the pan and stir in the chopped onion. Fry for about 5 minutes, or until soft, translucent and lightly browned. Stir in the garlic and ginger paste and fry for another 30 seconds and then add the ground spices. Mix well so that the onions are nicely coated and then add the beef stock or water, shatkora rinds and naga pickle and simmer for 5–10 minutes, or until you are happy with the sauce consistency. It should not be too wet.

Stir in the quartered tomato and fried doner meat. Add salt to taste and garnish with the chopped coriander. This spicy doner mixture is delicious served wrapped in hot rotis or naans, topped with salad and squirted with some kebab-shop sauces.

CHICKEN KARAHI
SERVES 4–6

I am always getting asked for karahi recipes. That's a difficult one because there are so many. A karahi curry is one that is cooked in a stainless steel or cast-iron karahi, but if all you have is a normal pan or better, a wok, use that. I love going to Lahore Kebab House in Whitechapel, London, and watching the chefs prepare their karahi curries over intense flame. In the West, karahi curries are often made with meat off the bone. Here I offer you a traditional version, as the bones add flavour to the sauce. This is also delicious with lamb: omit the first step and use a batch of cooked Peshawari namak mandi (see page 44) instead of the chicken. Using lamb that is already cooked means it has more time to become meltingly tender.

PREP TIME: 15 MINS
COOKING TIME: 35 MINS

1.5kg (3lb 5oz) skinless whole chicken, cut into 20 pieces
1 tsp salt, plus extra to taste
70ml (¼ cup) melted ghee or rapeseed (canola) oil
2 tbsp garlic and ginger paste (see page 169)
6 tomatoes
Approx. 250ml (1 cup) water or chicken stock
1 tbsp ground cumin
1 tbsp ground coriander
1 tbsp Kashmiri chilli powder
½ tsp ground turmeric
1 tsp ground black pepper
1 tbsp garam masala (see page 168)
8 green bird's eye chillies
4 tbsp julienned ginger
1 tsp dried fenugreek leaves (kasoori methi)
4 tbsp chopped coriander (cilantro)
Butter or ghee, to taste (optional)
Single (light) cream, to taste (optional)

Sprinkle the chicken pieces with the salt. Heat the oil or ghee (if you like a rich, buttery flavour to your curry, use ghee – if not, use oil) in a large karahi or wok over a high heat. When visibly hot, throw in the salted chicken pieces and fry for about 10 minutes, or until lightly browned in places.

Stir in the garlic and ginger paste and mix well so that it coats the chicken. Add the whole tomatoes and continue cooking and stirring until they become really soft and the skin starts to peel away, about 8 minutes. As the tomatoes become softer, remove their skins and discard. Mash the tomatoes in the pan with your spoon or spatula and add enough of the water (or stock, if you have it) to cover the bottom.

Bring the mixture to a simmer and then add the cumin, ground coriander, chilli powder, turmeric, black pepper and garam masala. Continue simmering, adding a little more water or stock if the curry is looking dry. If you add too much by mistake, just cook it down until the excess liquid evaporates.

At this point you should have an amazing-looking curry with a thick tomato sauce. Add the whole chillies and stir well to combine. Stir in most of the julienned ginger, then sprinkle the dried fenugreek leaves (kasoori methi) over the curry and check for seasoning, adding salt to taste. If you used oil and want a more buttery flavour, add a knob of ghee or butter to the pan. Some chefs add cream, too – I prefer mine without, but add a dash or two to taste if you like. Garnish with the remaining julienned ginger and the chopped coriander before serving.

CHICKEN SALI CURRY
SERVES 4

This is a Parsi curry that I have enjoyed many times at restaurants in Mumbai. It's such a simple curry to cook, which makes it perfect for cooking outdoors. The word *sali* refers to the fried matchstick potatoes that are piled high on top before serving. You could just buy ready-made sali, but they're easy to make yourself. Matchstick fried potatoes can be found at most large supermarkets.

PREP TIME: 15 MINS
COOKING TIME: 25 MINS

90ml (generous ⅓ cup) rapeseed (canola) oil
5 black peppercorns
5 green cardamom pods, lightly bruised
1 tsp cumin seeds
2.5cm (1in) cinnamon stick
5 cloves
2 red onions, very finely chopped
2 tbsp garlic and ginger paste (see page 169)
2 large tomatoes, diced
1 tbsp Kashmiri chilli powder
1 tbsp ground cumin
1 tbsp ground coriander
½ tsp ground turmeric
1kg (2lb 4oz) skinless whole chicken, cut into 10 pieces
70ml (¼ cup) tomato purée (see page 169)
1 tsp sugar (optional)
1 tbsp white wine or cider vinegar (optional)
4 handfuls of sali (fried matchstick potatoes), shop-bought or homemade (see opposite)
3 tbsp finely chopped coriander (cilantro)
Salt, to taste

Heat the oil in a karahi or wok over a high heat. When visibly hot, throw in the black peppercorns, cardamom pods, cumin seeds, cinnamon stick and cloves. Stir for about 30 seconds and then add the chopped red onions. Fry for about 8 minutes, or until the onions are a deep golden brown. Be sure to stir regularly so that the onions cook evenly. When they are caramelized and smelling amazing, add the garlic and ginger paste and stir for about 30 seconds. Now add the diced tomatoes and the ground spices and stir well to combine.

Place the chicken pieces in the pan and add just enough water to cover. About 250ml (1 cup) should do the job. Stir in the tomato purée and bring to a simmer. Cook for about 15 minutes, or until the chicken is cooked through and coated with a thick sauce.

The finished sauce should be slightly tangy and sweet. You can adjust the flavour by stirring in the sugar or vinegar, or both. Season with salt to taste. To serve, divide the curry between four serving bowls and garnish with a good handful of sali per serving and the chopped coriander (cilantro).

TO MAKE HOMEMADE SALI

Peel 4 potatoes and slice into matchsticks. Add to a large bowl of cold water and swirl around to remove any excess starch, then drain and dry completely with paper towels. Heat about 10cm (4in) rapeseed (canola) or peanut oil over a high heat until the oil reaches 180°C (355°F). Fry in small batches (about 1 large handful each) for 2½–3½ minutes, or until crisp and golden brown. It is important to fry in small batches to maintain the heat of the oil. Transfer the cooked sali to paper towels to drain any excess oil.

LAHORI CHARGHA
SERVES 3–4

Lahori chargha is seriously the best fried chicken I have ever eaten. First the chicken is marinated, then it is steamed until cooked through and finally it is shallow-fried. The end result is really juicy and out-of-this-world amazing. Yes, this recipe does take some work, but I promise you will want to make it again and again. Lahori chargha, which is often cooked at outdoor food stalls over fire, is a real party piece. It's also safe for serving to a crowd because the chicken is cooked through before adding it to the oil. You can double or triple the recipe if you want to serve more people. Of course, you could easily cook this indoors but it's a favourite at my family barbecues and a lot less messy.

PREP TIME: 15 MINS, PLUS MARINATING TIME
COOKING TIME: 1 HOUR

1.5kg (3lb 5oz) skinless whole chicken
1 tsp salt
Juice of 1 lemon
Rapeseed (canola) oil, for frying
Green chutney (see page 162) or raita, to serve

FOR THE MARINADE
1 blade mace
3 green bird's eye chillies, roughly chopped
5 garlic cloves, roughly chopped
2.5cm (1in) piece of ginger, peeled and julienned
1 tsp salt
1 tsp dried red chilli flakes
1 tbsp Kashmiri chilli powder
1 tsp ground coriander
1 tsp ground cumin
1 tsp chaat masala (see page 168), plus extra to serve
1 tsp amchoor powder (dried mango powder)
½ tsp ground black pepper
½ tsp ground turmeric
250g (1 cup) Greek yoghurt, whisked

Use a sharp chef's knife to make shallow slits all over the chicken and then rub the chicken with the salt and lemon juice. Set aside while you make the marinade.

Using a pestle and mortar, pound the mace into a powder and then add the green chillies, garlic cloves and ginger and continue pounding until you have a fine paste. This could also be done in a spice grinder. Pour this mixture into a large bowl and whisk in the remaining marinade ingredients. Rub the marinade all over and inside the chicken, being sure to get it right into the slits you made. Cover and leave to marinate in the fridge for at least 5 hours, or overnight, turning from time to time.

When ready to cook, prepare a direct heat fire (see page 10). When the coals are white-hot, place a steamer pan half-filled with water on the cooking grate and bring to a boil. Once boiling, place the marinated chicken in the steamer, cover and cook for 40 minutes. Remove from the heat.

Meanwhile, half-fill a large, deep frying pan or wok with the oil. The oil will need to come halfway up the chicken when it is lowered into it to cook. Once the oil has reached 175°C (350°F), carefully add the chicken breast side up and fry for 5–7 minutes, or until nice and crispy. Using some strong tongs, carefully turn the chicken to cook the other side for a further 5–7 minutes. The chicken is ready when you are happy with the colour and crispiness.

Transfer to paper towels to soak up any excess oil and serve immediately sprinkled with a little more chaat masala and green chutney and/or a good raita.

Left: Smoked chana dhal (page 145)
Right: Lahori chargha

CHICKEN GHEE ROAST
SERVES 4

South Indian ghee roast is awesome! Don't let the amount of ghee scare you off. It's called ghee roast, after all, and sometimes it's good to indulge in the better things in life. Although this is a chicken recipe, it's all about that ghee sauce. You could substitute prawns (shrimp), vegetables like cauliflower or broccoli, paneer... whatever sounds good, do it.

PREP TIME: 30 MINS
COOKING TIME: 30 MINS

8 skinless chicken thighs, cut in 2–3 pieces
Juice of 1 lemon
1 tbsp garlic and ginger paste (see page 169)
1 tsp ground turmeric
2 tsp Kashmiri chilli powder
2 tbsp Greek yoghurt
12 dried Kashmiri chillies
2 tsp cumin seeds
2 tbsp coriander seeds
2 tsp black peppercorns
½ tsp fenugreek seeds
2 tbsp tamarind pulp or 1 tbsp tamarind paste
12 garlic cloves
125ml (½ cup) melted ghee
30 fresh or frozen curry leaves
½ tsp sugar (more or less to taste)
½ tsp garam masala (see page 168)
Salt, to taste

Put the chicken pieces into a mixing bowl with the lemon juice, garlic and ginger paste, turmeric, chilli powder and yoghurt and mix well with your hands. Set aside to marinate while you prepare the curry paste.

Roast the dried chillies over a medium heat in a dry frying pan, stirring regularly. The idea is to soften the chillies, not darken them. As the chillies become fragrant, pour in the remaining dry spices and toast until warm to the touch and fragrant but not smoking. Transfer to a plate to cool.

Once cooled, blend to a fine powder in a spice grinder or food processor. Add the tamarind pulp or paste and garlic and just enough water to form a deep red paste. It should be slightly thick, but if yours is runny, no worries, you'll just need to cook it down longer.

Place a high-sided frying pan, wok or karahi over a high heat and add 5 tablespoons of the ghee to the pan. When hot, add the chicken pieces and stir them around to coat with the ghee so that none of the marinade sticks to the pan. You will need to stir continuously for about 5 minutes until the chicken is almost cooked through and the moisture from the chicken has released to start forming the sauce.

Transfer the chicken pieces to a plate and add the curry paste to the pan. Continue simmering and stirring so that the sauce thickens but doesn't burn. Simmer for about 5 minutes then swirl in the remaining ghee.

Return the chicken and any cooking juices from the plate to the pan and stir into the sauce. Stir the chicken continuously until the sauce is clinging to the chicken pieces. Stir in the curry leaves. Season with salt and sugar to taste and garnish with the garam masala before serving.

Left: Roasted vegetable fried rice (page 148)
Right: Chicken ghee roast

NOT JUST ANOTHER BUTTER CHICKEN RECIPE
SERVES 4-6

My original butter chicken recipe in *The Curry Guy* was similar to what you find at many Indian restaurants in the UK. Having now tried butter chicken many times at restaurants in India, I noticed some differences: one obvious one was the use of mustard oil and chaat masala or black salt in the marinade for the chicken; another was that the sauces had a lot more butter in them. The recipe below provides a different way of making tandoori chicken – delicious on its own or added to another curry sauce – as well as a sauce that is much closer to what I experienced on my travels.

PREP TIME: 25 MINS, PLUS MARINATING TIME
COOKING TIME: 15 MINS

70ml (¼ cup) mustard oil
2kg (4½lb) skinless chicken, cut into small pieces and scored
Juice of 1 large lemon
2 tsp salt
2 tbsp garlic and ginger paste (see page 169)
175ml (¾ cup) Greek yoghurt, whisked
1½ tbsp Kashmiri chilli powder
1 tsp ground cumin
1 tsp ground coriander
½ tsp turmeric
1 tsp chaat masala (see page 168)

FOR THE SAUCE

800g (1lb 12oz) tinned (canned) chopped tomatoes
20 raw cashew nuts
2 large red onions, roughly chopped
2 tbsp rapeseed (canola) oil
100g (3½oz) butter
2 generous tbsp garlic and ginger paste (see page 169)
2 tsp Kashmiri chilli powder or paprika
1 tsp ground cumin
1 tsp ground coriander
175ml (¾ cup) double (heavy) cream
1 tbsp dried fenugreek leaves
½ tsp garam masala
Salt, to taste

Start by heating the mustard oil to smoking point, then remove from the heat and allow to cool to room temperature.

Put the chicken pieces into a large mixing bowl and add the lemon juice, salt and garlic and ginger paste. Whisk the now-cooled mustard oil, the yoghurt and ground spices together until smooth. Pour this marinade over the chicken and mix well to ensure the chicken is totally coated. Cover and leave to marinate in the fridge for 1 hour, or ideally overnight.

When ready to cook, prepare a direct heat fire (see page 10). Rub as much marinade off the chicken as you can, retaining the marinade for the sauce. Thread the chicken onto skewers. (You could also cook the chicken on a lightly greased cooking grate.) When the coals are white-hot and it is uncomfortable to hold your hand 5cm (2in) above the grill for more than 2 seconds, you're ready to cook.

Place the chicken skewers over the fire and cook for 5 minutes, or until nicely charred on one side. Rotate the skewers and cook for a further 5 minutes. Transfer to a plate to rest while you make the butter sauce.

Put the tomatoes and cashew nuts into a blender or food processor and blend until smooth. Transfer to a bowl and set aside. Next, blend the onions with a little water until smooth. Place a karahi, wok or large saucepan on the grate over the hottest part of the fire and add the oil and half the butter. When sizzling, pour in the blended onions and fry for 6–7 minutes, stirring regularly. Stir in the garlic and ginger paste along with the chilli powder or paprika, ground cumin and ground coriander and fry for a further 30 seconds.

Add the blended tomatoes and cashew nuts and stir well to combine and then add the cooked chicken and reserved marinade. Bring to a simmer and stir in the cream and remaining butter. To finish, add the dried fenugreek leaves by rubbing them between your fingers. Season with salt to taste and sprinkle with the garam masala before serving.

CHICKEN DUM BIRYANI
SERVES 6–8

This is an amazing, classic biryani recipe that has never failed me. Sometimes I find biryanis a bit dry, but that's not the case here. The onions can be fried a couple of days ahead of time and stored in an airtight container, or you could use shop-bought fried onions.

PREP TIME: 30 MINS, PLUS SOAKING TIME
COOKING TIME: 1 HOUR

FOR THE SAUCE
3 tbsp rapeseed (canola) oil
1 tsp cumin seeds
1 tsp black peppercorns
4 green cardamom pods, bruised
2.5cm (1in) cinnamon stick
1 star anise
3 generous tbsp garlic, ginger
  and chilli paste (see page 169)
3 onions, thinly sliced and fried
400g (14oz) tinned (canned)
  chopped tomatoes
1½ tbsp Kashmiri chilli power
½ tsp ground turmeric
1 tsp ground coriander
1 tbsp garam masala (see page 168)
150g (5½oz) natural yoghurt
500g (1lb 2oz) potatoes, peeled
  and cut into bite-size pieces
1 whole skinless chicken, cut
  into about 10 pieces
Salt, to taste

FOR THE RICE
600g (3 cups) basmati rice
3 tbsp salt
2 Indian bay leaves
1 tsp black peppercorns
3 green cardamom pods, bruised
2.5cm (1in) cinnamon stick
1 star anise
1 small bunch of coriander
  (cilantro), leaves finely
  chopped
1 small bunch of mint, leaves
  finely chopped
125ml (½ cup) melted ghee
A pinch of saffron, infused in
  4 tbsp hot milk

First wash the rice. Put the rice into a bowl and cover with cold water. Swirl the water; it will become milky from the rice starch. Pour the water out and add fresh water. Repeat until the water is almost clear – you will need to do this several times. Cover with water once more and leave to soak for 1 hour.

Now start the sauce. Heat the oil in a 6-litre (6 US quart) pot over a multi-level direct heat fire (see page 10). When visibly hot, stir in the whole spices and infuse into the oil for about 30 seconds. Add the garlic, ginger and chilli paste and half the fried onions and fry for about 30 seconds. Stir in the chopped tomatoes and bring to a simmer.

Next add the ground spices and 750ml (3 cups) water and simmer for 3 minutes. Stir in the yoghurt and the potato pieces and continue simmering for 5 minutes, or until the potatoes are about half cooked.

Add the chicken and simmer for about 8 minutes, or until it is about 80% cooked through. Season with salt to taste and continue simmering while you prepare the rice.

Fill a large saucepan with 4 litres (4 US quarts) water, add the salt, bay leaves and aromatic spices and bring to a boil over a high heat. Add the soaked rice and simmer for about 6 minutes, or until par-cooked. Using a sieve or large slotted spoon, transfer half the rice to the biryani pan, covering the sauce with it. The rice might look like it's drowning at this stage – that's fine. Sprinkle with half the coriander (cilantro) and mint leaves, a quarter of the remaining fried onions, half the melted ghee and half the saffron milk mixture. Strain the remaining rice and transfer it to the biryani pan to cover, then sprinkle with the remaining fried onions, coriander, mint, melted ghee and saffron milk.

The biryani needs to steam in an air-tight pan. You could make up some dough to do this (see page 112) or just wrap the top of the pan tightly with foil and place the lid on top. Cook the covered biryani for 5 minutes over a high heat and then transfer to a lower heat to cook slowly for a further 25 minutes.

I suggest removing the lid at the table as the aroma is incredible. Carefully stir the biryani from the bottom before serving – the green chutney on page 162 is a good accompaniment.

CHICKEN TAWA
SERVES 4–6

At street-food stalls, this hugely popular Lahori chicken recipe is cooked on a massive plancha or griddle. Home cooks usually cook it on a tawa, a flat pan used a lot for making flat breads, hence the name of the recipe. You could do this, too, but I prefer to use a heavy plancha placed on the grate over the fire. The chicken needs to be cooked before it hits the plancha; in this recipe it is simply grilled over direct heat. I often serve this wrapped in a chapati – if doing this, I use chicken tikka instead of chicken on the bone.

PREP TIME: 15 MINS, PLUS MARINATING TIME
COOKING TIME: 25 MINS

8 whole skinless chicken legs
4 limes, quartered
½ tsp salt, plus extra to taste
2 tbsp garlic and ginger paste (see page 169)
90ml (generous ⅓ cup) rapeseed (canola) oil, plus extra for greasing
5 green bird's eye chillies, thinly sliced
2 red spur chillies, thinly sliced
5cm (2in) piece of ginger, julienned
30g (1 packed cup) coriander (cilantro), finely chopped
2 tbsp butter
½ tsp garam masala (see page 168)
Rotis, to serve

FOR THE MARINADE

250g (1 cup) natural yoghurt
125ml (½ cup) single (light) cream
3 tbsp distilled white vinegar
4 tbsp garlic paste or minced garlic
2 tbsp Kashmiri chilli powder
1 tbsp dried red chilli flakes (optional)
2 tbsp ground coriander
1 tbsp ground cumin
1 tbsp chaat masala (optional; see page 168)

Score each chicken leg about six times and put in a mixing bowl. Squeeze over the juice of one of the limes, add the salt and garlic and ginger paste and stir well to combine.

Next, whisk together all the marinade ingredients in a bowl until smooth, adding salt to taste. Take 3 tablespoons of the marinade and rub it into the chicken. Place the chicken in one bowl and the remaining marinade in another. Cover and place both bowls in the fridge. Marinate the chicken for at least 30 minutes, or overnight. Remove the chicken from the fridge about 30 minutes before you want to start cooking.

Prepare a direct heat fire (see page 10). When the coals are white-hot and it is uncomfortable to hold your hand 5cm (2in) above the grill for more than 2 seconds, you're ready to cook. Brush the cooking grate with a little oil. Place the chicken on the grate and cook for 10 minutes, or until cooked through, turning from time to time. Transfer the cooked chicken to a plate.

Place your tawa, plancha or pan on the grate. Allow the cooking surface to get good and hot and then add the oil. When the oil is visibly hot, add the cooked chicken and immediately spoon over some of the reserved marinade. Turn the chicken over and add more of the marinade. As you do this, the marinade will sizzle on the hot surface.

Cut into the chicken in places with your spatula and continue turning the chicken and adding more marinade. Just before adding the last bit of marinade, sprinkle generously with the chillies, lime wedges, julienned ginger and coriander (cilantro). Stir well and add the butter, then sprinkle over the garam masala. When the butter has melted into the sauce, your job is done. Serve with hot rotis, which can be heated up on the tawa or plancha in any remaining sauce.

By the way, that marinade/sauce tastes incredible. Sometimes I make more and heat it up while the chicken rests and serve it stirred into the chicken. That, or hold some of the original marinade back to heat up and serve with the chicken.

GOAT RAAN
SERVES 4-6

Goat meat is so underrated! It might still be difficult to come by, but a good butcher will get it for you. Make things easy on yourself and ask your butcher to remove all the surface fat. Goat can be tough, but this recipe ensures tender and perfectly cooked meat. You could substitute leg of lamb if goat isn't your thing, though. This is a spicy one – just reduce the amount of chillies and chilli powder if you would like it less hot.

PREP TIME: 20 MINS, PLUS MARINATING TIME
COOKING TIME: 3½ HOURS

1 goat leg, approx. 1.5kg (3lb 5oz), surface fat removed
5 garlic cloves, thinly sliced
80ml (⅓ cup) melted ghee
250ml (1 cup) beef, lamb or goat stock
1 tsp chaat masala (optional; see page 168)
Flaky sea salt and freshly ground black pepper, to taste

FOR THE MARINADE

4 tbsp garlic, ginger and chilli paste (see page 169)
1 tsp cumin
1 tbsp garam masala
3 tbsp Kashmiri chilli powder (more or less to taste)
Juice of 3 limes
200g (generous ¾ cup) Greek yoghurt
Salt, to taste

In a bowl, whisk together the marinade ingredients until smooth. Next, using a sharp knife, make deep slits all over the goat leg, then make small holes and fill them with the garlic. Rub the marinade all over the leg and deep into the flesh. Cover and leave to marinate in the fridge for at least 6 hours, or up to 72 hours.

When ready to cook, bring the goat leg to room temperature and set up your barbecue for indirect heat cooking (see page 9). You are aiming for a cooking temperature of 180°C (355°F). Rub off as much of the marinade as you can and retain it for later. Place the goat leg on a roasting pan, cover loosely with foil and put on the cooler side of the barbecue to cook for 3 hours. Baste it with a little of the ghee from time to time (you may not need all of it) and be sure to keep the coals topped up to maintain the heat. After 3 hours, the meat should be falling off the bone, but this is barbecue! It's ready when it's ready so cook longer if necessary.

When cooked to your liking, transfer the meat to a plate and spread out the coals for direct heat cooking. Place the roasting pan with all the cooking juices over the fire and add the stock. Let this come to a simmer, then whisk in the reserved marinade 1 tablespoon at a time. Simmer until you are happy with the consistency, then season with salt to taste. I like it quite thick and spicy, mildly salty with a good hit of sourness from the lime juice, but you could and should adjust this to your own taste. When the sauce is looking and tasting delicious, cover it and keep warm. Place the goat leg on the grill and char it all over until blackened to your liking; this should only take a couple of minutes.

Transfer to a cutting board and allow to rest for about 20 minutes before slicing. Cut the meat off the bone and then slice thinly against the grain, or, if it is tender enough, just tear the meat off to serve. Top with the sauce and sprinkle with the chaat masala, if using. Add flaky sea salt and black pepper to taste.

MUTTON PAANI FRY
SERVES 6

Pani or paani means water in Hindi and Urdu. This is a dry-fried mutton curry that is cooked in water without oil. Believe me, you won't miss the oil one bit! You could also use lamb or goat in this recipe, as 'mutton' often refers to goat meat in the Indian subcontinent. Although this recipe is perfect as it is, there is another option, which is to fry the cooked mutton in ghee to make it super crispy – see the note below.

PREP TIME: 10 MINS
COOKING TIME: 1 HOUR 20 MINS

1kg (2lb 4oz) mutton, lamb or goat leg on the bone, cut into bite-size pieces
4 dried Kashmiri chillies, torn into 3 pieces
4 green bird's eye chillies, roughly chopped
8 garlic cloves, smashed
1 tsp black peppercorns
1½ tsp salt
1 tbsp ground cumin
½ tsp ground turmeric
1 tsp Kashmiri chilli powder
70ml (¼ cup) melted ghee (optional: see Note)
½ tsp garam masala (see page 168)
Lemon wedges, to serve

Prepare a direct heat fire (see page 10). Put a large karahi or saucepan on the cooking grate over the hottest part of the fire and add the mutton. Add all the remaining ingredients except for the garam masala and lemon wedges. Pour in about 2 litres (8 cups) water to cover the meat completely. Bring to a rolling simmer and leave to cook for 1 hour.

After 1 hour, the liquid should have reduced by more than half and the mutton will be looking and smelling amazing. Give it all a good stir and continue cooking until you only have about 125ml (½ cup) of sauce in the pan. The amount of time this takes will depend on the heat of your fire, but it should be about 30 minutes. Much of the remaining sauce will be the rendered fat from the mutton.

Check the mutton for doneness. It should be really tender and falling off the bone. If not, add a little more water and continue cooking until it is. Add the garam masala and check for seasoning, adding more salt if needed. Serve with the lemon wedges.

NOTE
Not counting calories? Try this: once cooked, remove the meat from the sauce, reserving the sauce. Place a large frying pan or karahi over the hottest part of the fire and add 70ml (¼ cup) melted ghee. When bubbling hot, fry the cooked mutton until crisp and nicely browned. A couple of minutes should do the trick. Pour the reserved sauce over the fried meat and serve.

CHAMPARAN MUTTON HANDI
SERVES 4

This mutton curry is traditionally cooked in a lidded clay pot called a handi, sealed shut with dough and placed right on the coals. It's one of my all-time favourites! The first time you make this, though, I recommend using a glass lid with a steam hole so you can see what's going on inside as it cooks. If you don't have a handi, use a heavy-based saucepan or cast-iron casserole dish. This is a dry curry that's perfect served with grilled roti, naans, chapatis or rice. Both finely chopped garlic and whole heads of garlic are added. If you are a big garlic fan like me, you will love the soft whole heads that you can squeeze into the curry or directly into your mouth!

PREP: 20 MINS
COOKING TIME: 50 MINS

125ml (½ cup) mustard oil, heated to smoking point and then cooled to room temperature
5cm (2in) cinnamon stick
6 green cardamom pods, bruised
3 black cardamom pods, bruised (optional)
2 Indian bay leaves
4 red onions, grated
10 garlic cloves, unpeeled but smashed and finely chopped
1½ tsp salt
1 tbsp Kashmiri chilli powder
½ tsp ground turmeric
2 tsp ground coriander
2 tsp ground cumin
1 tsp ground fennel
2 tsp garam masala (see page 168)
6 green bird's eye chillies, slit down the middle
4 whole heads of garlic
900g (2lb) diced mutton/lamb leg on the bone
150g (1 cup) plain (all-purpose) flour
3 generous tbsp melted ghee (optional but recommended!)
Rice or naans, to serve

Once you have heated the mustard oil to smoking point and then cooled to room temperature, you can infuse this with the spices. Pour the oil into a saucepan, place over a high heat and add the whole spices and bay leaves. Infuse for about 30 seconds, then remove from the heat.

Prepare a direct heat fire (see page 10). While it is heating up, pour half of the infused mustard oil into a clay handi, casserole dish or metal saucepan with a lid. Add the grated onions, chopped garlic, salt and the ground spices. Stir well. Add the green chillies, whole heads of garlic and the diced mutton/lamb. Pour the remaining mustard oil over it all and stir well so that everything is coated evenly.

To make the dough seal, simply mix the flour with enough water to form a soft dough. You might need more or less flour depending on the size of your pot – this won't be eaten so there's no need to get too precise with it! Roll the dough into a long rope shape and run it around the top of the pot, then place the lid on top, pushing it down to seal.

Place the sealed pot directly on the hottest part of the coals and leave to cook for 3 minutes. Shake the pot to move the ingredients around inside and then return to the cooler part of the coals. Every 10 minutes or so, pick up the pot and give it a few good, hard shakes. This will help ensure that the meat cooks without sticking to the bottom of the pot. Each time you do this, you will hear more juices being splashed around inside.

After about 50 minutes, the meat inside will be fall-off-the-bone tender and the heads of garlic will be squeezably soft. Take the pot to the table, remove the lid and stir in the melted ghee, if using. This is a real showpiece and the aroma is amazing. Serve with rice or naans.

STAFF PANGASIUS CURRY
SERVES 4

Few recipes have surprised me as much as this one. Just after starting my blog in 2010, I was invited to a local curry house to try some of their staff curries. The idea of seared pangasius with a spinach sauce sounded interesting but I didn't think I would like it as much as I did. It was amazing. If you can't find pangasius, basa is a good substitute. This is one you've simply got to try. Cooking it on a barbecue gives it a more rustic flavour that I really love. This is spicy, so reduce the amount of chilli powder and naga pickle if you prefer.

PREP TIME: 10 MINS
COOKING TIME: 15 MINS

70ml (¼ cup) rapeseed (canola) oil
1 tsp panch phoran
1 tbsp garlic paste or finely chopped garlic
10 fresh curry leaves
1 small onion, finely chopped
1 small cinnamon stick
1 Indian bay leaf
2 tsp ground turmeric
2 tsp curry powder or garam masala (see page 168)
1 tsp Kashmiri chilli powder
200g (7oz) baby spinach leaves, shredded
1 tsp dried fenugreek leaves (kasoori methi)
2–4 green bird's eye chillies, finely chopped
2 tsp shatkora pickle
3 tsp naga pickle (I use Mr Naga brand)
4 pangasius or basa fillets
Salt, to taste

Prepare a direct heat fire (see page 10). When the coals have ashed over and it is uncomfortable to hold your hand 5cm (2in) above the grill for more than 2 seconds, you're ready to cook.

Heat 3 tablespoons of the oil in a saucepan over a medium-high heat. Add the panch phoran to the hot oil and fry for about 30 seconds, then add the garlic and fry for about 1 minute until golden, but be careful not to burn it.

Add the curry leaves and finely chopped onion and fry for about 5 minutes, or until the onion is soft and translucent. Add a pinch of salt and then throw in the cinnamon stick, bay leaf and about 125ml (½ cup) water. Bring to a simmer and add half the turmeric, the curry powder or garam masala and chilli powder. Cook for a further 5 minutes.

Add the shredded spinach and another 125ml (½ cup) water and cook until the spinach has reduced to a paste. Add the dried fenugreek leaves (kasoori methi), chopped green chillies, shatkora pickle and naga pickle, then mix everything through and leave to simmer as you prepare the fish.

Pour the remaining oil into a bowl. Dust the fish fillets with the remaining turmeric and a little salt and then coat them with the oil. Place a frying pan over a high heat and when visibly hot, add the fish. Fry until cooked through on both sides – about 3 minutes each side should be enough, but check with the point of a knife to make sure it is cooked through.

Place the fish fillets on a heated serving plate and top with the spinach mixture to serve.

KERALAN FISH ROAST
SERVES 4

Unless you live near a good Asian fish market, you might find it difficult to find silver pomfret, a delicious fish that is hugely popular in southern India. I have included it here as I love the flavour and buttery texture, but if you can't get it, you can substitute another fish such as bass, snapper, bream or lemon sole. You will need a pan that is large enough to hold all the fish at the same time.

If it's more convenient, you could blacken the tomatoes and prepare the marinade inside; simply add the tomatoes to a large, dry frying pan and place over a high heat.

PREP TIME: 15 MINS
COOKING TIME: 15 MINS

5 tomatoes
50g (¼ cup) chana dhal
250ml (1 cup) coconut oil, plus
    extra for greasing and frying
1 tsp ground cumin
5 garlic cloves, smashed and
    roughly chopped
3–6 green bird's eye chillies
3 tbsp chopped coriander
    (cilantro)
1½ tbsp Kashmiri chilli powder
    (more or less to taste)
1 tsp chaat masala (see page 168)
1 tsp amchoor (dried mango
    powder)
1 tsp lemon juice
4 x 400–500g (14oz–1lb 2oz)
    silver pomfret
60 fresh or frozen curry leaves
Salt, to taste

Prepare a direct heat fire (see page 10). When the coals have ashed over and it is uncomfortable to hold your hand 5cm (2in) above the grill for more than 2 seconds, you're ready to cook. Lightly grease the cooking grate with oil and then place the tomatoes on top. Cook, turning regularly, until blackened all over; this will take about 10 minutes and gives the tomatoes a delicious smoky flavour. Set aside to cool slightly, then dice.

Next, toast the chana dhal in a large, dry frying pan over a medium heat for about 5 minutes, stirring regularly, until toasted and golden. Transfer to a plate to cool.

Meanwhile, add 1 teaspoon of oil to the same pan and stir in the cumin and garlic. Fry for about 1 minute, then add the green chillies, coriander (cilantro), toasted chana dhal and diced charred tomatoes and bring to a simmer. Add the chilli powder, chaat masala and amchoor (dried mango powder). Stir well and take off the heat to cool slightly. Once cooled, blend the mixture to a smooth paste with a stick blender. Stir in the lemon juice and season with salt to taste.

Clean out the pan, return to a high heat and add the 250ml (1 cup) coconut oil. When sizzling, dip the whole fish into the paste so that they are coated all over and then lay them in the hot oil. Fry for a couple of minutes and then flip the fish over to fry the other side. As the fish are frying, baste them with the remaining paste and splash them with the hot coconut oil. You might want to flip the fish again and do the same on the other side. Keep splashing the fish with the oil and dabbing them with more of the paste, adding more oil if needed. They should be swimming in hot coconut oil.

When the fish is lightly charred and the aroma is making everyone hungry, sprinkle the curry leaves over the fish. You'll know when the fish is ready because it will look too good to leave in the pan a second longer! Carefully transfer the fish to a platter, along with any paste left in the pan, scatter over the curry leaves and dig in!

CURRY-STUFFED NAAN
SERVES 4–6

Any dry curry can be stuffed into a naan, but the most popular version is keema naan. How large you make your curry-stuffed naans will be down to the size of your barbecue. I once used a small portable kettle barbecue and made small naans, cooked one at a time. No one complained about the wait, though, as they were brought to the table sizzling hot and delicious.

PREP TIME: 15 MINS
COOKING TIME: 50 MINS

3 tbsp rapeseed (canola) oil
2 Indian bay leaves
5cm (2in) cinnamon stick or cassia bark
1 tsp cumin seeds
4 green cardamom pods, lightly bruised
1 onion, finely chopped
1 tbsp garlic and ginger paste (see page 169)
1 tbsp tandoori masala (see page 167)
1 tbsp garam masala (see page 168)
½ tsp ground turmeric
2 tbsp tomato purée (see page 169)
500g (1lb 2oz) minced (ground) lamb, beef or chicken
1 tsp dried fenugreek leaves (kasoori methi)
3 tbsp finely chopped coriander (cilantro)
Salt, to taste

FOR THE NAANS
1 batch grilled naan dough (see page 151)
80g (⅓ cup) Greek yoghurt, whisked
3 tbsp melted ghee
4 tbsp finely chopped coriander (cilantro)

Heat the oil in a saucepan or deep frying pan over a medium-high heat until small bubbles appear, then stir in the bay leaves, cinnamon stick, cumin seeds and cardamom pods. After about 30 seconds the oil will become fragrant. When this happens, toss in the onion and give it a good stir. Fry until soft and translucent, about 5 minutes.

Add the garlic and ginger paste and let it sizzle for another minute or so, then add the ground spices and tomato purée followed by the minced (ground) meat and 200ml (generous ¾ cup) water. Stir quickly so that the meat takes on the consistency of thick porridge and then keep cooking for about 20 minutes, or until the water has mostly evaporated. The finished keema should be moist but not saucy. Remove the bay leaves, cinnamon stick and cardamom pods. Stir in the dried fenugreek leaves (kasoori methi) and coriander (cilantro) and season with salt. Transfer to a plate to cool.

When ready to cook the naans, set up your barbecue for indirect heat cooking (see page 9). Close the lid and open the bottom and top vents completely. You're aiming for a temperature of between 180°C (355°F) and 230°C (455°F).

Depending on the size of your grill, divide the dough into 2, 4 or 6 dough balls. Roll them out into round discs about 9mm (⅓in) thick and then pile them high with the keema mixture. Start by adding 3 generous tablespoons of the keema mixture. If you think you can get more on there, do it! Wrap the dough around the meat and then seal it shut with your fingers. Flip the dough parcels over, sealed side down, and roll them out on a couple of baking trays into slightly larger circles. Using the handle of a wooden spoon or similar, make indentations all over the top, creating small holes so that you can see some of the keema inside. Brush the tops with the whisked yoghurt.

When the barbecue is up to heat, place the baking trays with the naans on top on the cooler side of the barbecue grate. Cook for 20 minutes, or until golden brown, then brush with the melted ghee and garnish with the chopped coriander (cilantro).

NOTE
These are also great cooked in a wood-fired oven. When I cook these in my pizza oven, I cook at about 350°C (650°F) for 3–4 minutes.

KEEMA RICE

SERVES 8

I decided to include this recipe after being asked so many times for a good recipe for keema rice. So that is what you'll get here! This is a great way to use up leftover rice, as the rice needs to be cold when it hits the pan, otherwise it could become mushy. If you're making the rice fresh, remember that rice doubles in weight when cooked, so you'll need 400g (2 cups) uncooked rice.

PREP TIME: 10 MINS
COOKING TIME: 15 MINS

600g (1lb 5oz) minced (ground) lamb
3 tbsp rapeseed (canola) oil or ghee
1 tsp panch phoran
2 onions, finely chopped
2 tbsp garlic and ginger paste (see page 169)
2 green bird's eye chillies, finely chopped
1 tsp ground cumin
1 tsp ground coriander
1 tsp garam masala (see page 168), plus extra to serve
1 tsp Kashmiri chilli powder
½ tsp ground turmeric
70ml (¼ cup) tomato purée (see page 169)
100g (½ cup) spinach
800g (4 cups) cold cooked basmati rice (see page 147)
Salt, to taste
Roasted onion raita (see page 161), to serve
Green chutney (see page 162), to serve

Start by preparing the minced (ground) meat. Put the meat in a bowl and stir in about 500ml (2 cups) water, until the meat is soupy and has the texture of thick porridge. Set aside.

Heat the oil or ghee in a karahi or large frying pan over a high heat. When visibly hot, add the panch phoran and fry for about 30 seconds, then add the chopped onions. Fry for about 7 minutes, or until soft, translucent and lightly browned. Add the garlic and ginger paste and chillies. Fry for a further minute and then stir in the ground spices followed by the minced lamb. Brown the meat for a couple of minutes and then add the tomato purée and spinach and stir in.

To finish, stir in the cold cooked rice. Season with salt and sprinkle with a little garam masala before serving with raita and/or green chutney.

BENGALI KATI ROLLS
SERVES 4

Back when my kids were young, we used to do a lot of camping. We cooked everything on our little portable barbecue. Then when I started my food blog in 2010 our cooking took a new course, with Indian food for breakfast, lunch and dinner. These Bengali kati rolls were almost always breakfast on our camping trips, often filled with leftover tandoori chicken. This famous street-food snack originated in Kolkata and was made with busy people in mind, providing a wrapped snack that they could eat on their way to and from work without making a mess.

PREP TIME: 20 MINS
COOKING TIME: 15 MINS

125ml (½ cup) rapeseed (canola) oil or melted ghee
4 large uncooked rotis, about 30cm (12in) diameter (see page 154), or shop-bought chapatis
4 eggs
Sauce of your choice, to serve (see Note)

FOR THE SALAD

1 cucumber, deseeded and cut into matchsticks or grated
1 red onion, thinly sliced
4 green bird's eye chillies, thinly sliced
1 tbsp rapeseed (canola) or olive oil
Salt or black salt and freshly ground black pepper, to taste

Start by making the salad. Combine the vegetables and chillies with the oil in a mixing bowl and season to taste. Set aside.

For the kati rolls, heat a tawa or frying pan over a high heat fire and add 3 tablespoons of the oil or ghee. When sizzling hot, place a roti in the pan and move it around so that the underside is nicely coated with the oil and it begins to bubble a little on top. Break an egg on top of the roti and move it around to scramble it over the surface of the bread, covering as much of it as you can. When the egg is about half cooked, flip the roti. When you do this, the uncooked egg will slide into the pan. Cover it with the roti quickly and move it around to coat. The roti is finished when it looks deliciously browned and bubbly in places. Transfer to a plate or pan to keep warm and repeat with the remaining rotis, adding more oil or ghee to the pan as required.

When the egg-coated rotis are all ready, quickly assemble them by topping with the salad and the sauce of your choice before rolling up like a burrito.

NOTE
The green chutney on page 162 is a firm favourite for these rolls, but I also like these with the kebab-shop sauces on page 165.

MUSHROOM BHAJI
SERVES 2

In the UK, mushroom bhaji is usually made with a base curry sauce. Not so in India. Here I show you a more traditional way by preparing this dish outdoors, which is a hugely popular way of cooking this vegan curry. You could just use standard button mushrooms for this, but if you can get your hands on some wild mushrooms, use them for even better flavour. You could also make this into a vegetable bhaji by reducing the quantity of mushrooms and adding different vegetables of your choice. This mushroom bhaji is delicious served over rice or wrapped up in a hot roti or paratha.

PREP TIME: 10 MINS
COOKING TIME: 10 MINS

3 tbsp rapeseed (canola) oil
250g (9oz) button mushrooms, sliced
1 large red onion, very finely chopped
1 generous tbsp garlic and ginger paste (see page 169)
½ red (bell) pepper, cut into matchsticks
1 generous tbsp garam masala (see page 168)
1 tsp Kashmiri chilli powder (more or less to taste)
½ tsp ground turmeric
2 large tomatoes, blended, or 125ml (½ cup) tomato purée (see page 169)
3 tbsp finely chopped coriander (cilantro)
2.5cm (1in) piece of ginger, peeled and julienned
Salt, to taste
Lemon wedges, to serve

Heat 2 tbsp of the oil in a karahi or frying pan over a high heat. When visibly hot, add the mushrooms and fry for 3–5 minutes until cooked through and well browned. Transfer to a plate and set aside.

Add the remaining oil to the pan and stir in the chopped onion. Fry for about 5 minutes until soft, lightly browned and translucent and then stir in the garlic and ginger paste and sliced red (bell) pepper. Fry for 30 seconds, then add the ground spices followed by the tomatoes. Bring to a simmer and then add 125ml (½ cup) water and bring to a simmer again.

Once the sauce has reduced down to your liking, return the fried mushrooms to the pan and stir well to combine. Add salt to taste and garnish with the chopped coriander (cilantro) and julienned ginger. Serve immediately with the lemon wedges for squeezing over.

SHAMI KEBAB BURGER
SERVES 4

Shami kebabs are delicious, melt-in-the-mouth kebabs that are great on their own with a good chutney but that also make one excellent burger. When served on their own, they are usually made quite small so that they can be picked up without falling apart. Here, I have made them big enough to fill a burger bun and then added all the additions you might expect in a good burger.

PREP TIME: 15 MINS, PLUS SOAKING TIME
COOKING TIME: 1 HOUR

4 tbsp ghee
5 dried Kashmiri chillies
1 tsp cumin seeds
2 Indian bay leaves (optional)
5 green cardamom pods, bruised so that the seeds are almost falling out
3 cloves
2.5cm (1in) cinnamon stick
5 garlic cloves, crushed and roughly chopped
2.5cm (1in) piece of ginger, peeled and roughly chopped
½ red onion, roughly chopped
1 tsp salt
½ tsp ground black pepper
600g (1lb 5oz) leg or shoulder of lamb or mutton, cut into bite-size chunks
80g (generous ½ cup) chana dhal, rinsed and soaked for 30 minutes

TO SERVE
8–10 green bird's eye chillies
Approx. 2 tbsp butter
4 burger buns
Kebab-shop garlic sauce (see page 165) or mayonnaise
Kebab-shop red chilli sauce (see page 165) or ketchup
Green chutney (see page 162)
Iceberg lettuce leaves
Sliced tomato
Sliced red onion
4 slices of cheese of your choice (optional)

The first part of this recipe can be done indoors on your hob if more convenient. Melt 2 tablespoons of the ghee in a frying pan over a high heat. When hot, stir in the dried chillies and whole spices. Let these infuse into the ghee for about 30 seconds and then add the garlic, ginger and red onion. Fry until the onion is soft, stirring often so the garlic doesn't burn. Stir in the salt, black pepper and the meat and fry briefly to brown the meat. This should only take a minute or so. Add the soaked chana dhal, then add 250ml (1 cup) water, or more if needed, to cover.

Cover and simmer for about 40 minutes, or until the water has almost evaporated and the meat is really tender. The meat should fall apart when tested with a fork. If not, add some more water and continue cooking until tender. Transfer to a plate to cool slightly and remove the bay leaves, cinnamon stick and cardamom pods.

Transfer the meat mixture to a food processor and blend to a smooth paste. It should have the consistency of wet clay. Divide into four equal-sized patties of a similar circumference to the burger buns you are using.

If you've not already done so, prepare a direct heat fire (see page 10). Char the green chillies either directly on the grill or in the pan, then set aside. Spread the butter over the buns and toast to your liking over the fire. Then spread each bun liberally with your chosen sauces and top with lettuce, tomato and red onion slices and a couple of charred chillies.

Melt the remaining ghee in the pan over direct heat and carefully add the shami patties. Fry until golden brown on the underside, about 2 minutes, then flip over. Be careful when flipping the patties or they will easily fall apart! The patties are already cooked so you just need to give them a crispy, brown exterior. Fry the other side until golden brown and top with cheese if you wish.

Place the shami patties on the salad-topped buns, add the tops and serve.

BEEF CHAPLI KEBAB BURGER
SERVES 6

This is a play on the famous beef chapli kebab, which is hugely popular in Pakistan and northern India. For that matter, they are quite popular at takeaways in the West now too! Classic beef chapli kebabs are formed into large patties and then deep-fried in beef fat until crispy (so good) but here I decided to skip the deep-frying and make smash burgers with the delicious meat mixture instead. Good-quality minced (ground) beef is key – I ask my butcher for a blend of skirt, chuck, short rib and brisket. I was going to suggest that the beef marrow in this recipe is optional but it's too good to leave out! Do find some and add to the mix – you'll be amazed by the flavour.

PREP TIME: 15 MINS
COOKING TIME: 15 MINS

2 red onions, grated
3 tbsp finely chopped coriander (cilantro)
2 tbsp garlic and ginger paste (see page 169)
3 green bird's eye chillies, very finely chopped
1 tbsp dried red chilli flakes
1 tsp Kashmiri chilli powder
1 tbsp cumin seeds, coarsely ground
1 tbsp coriander seeds, coarsely ground
1 tsp garam masala (see page 168)
1 tsp ground black pepper
½ tsp salt, plus extra to taste
2 tbsp gram (chickpea) flour
800g (1lb 12oz) minced (ground) beef (preferably 20% fat)
200g (7oz) beef bone marrow, finely chopped
3 tomatoes, peeled, deseeded and finely chopped
2 tbsp rapeseed (canola) oil
12 slices of burger cheese

TO FINISH
Green chutney (see page 162)
6 burger buns, buttered and toasted
Iceberg lettuce leaves
Sliced tomato
Sliced onion

Put the grated onions into the centre of a piece of muslin (cheesecloth) and squeeze out as much of the juice as you can (reserve the juice to use in the minced doner kebabs on page 92, if you like). Put the grated onion into a large bowl and add the ingredients up to and including the minced (ground) beef, then mix together with your hands. You really want to break the meat down so knead it for about 10 minutes until the mince is super-fine and the ingredients are well combined.

Work the chopped bone marrow into the meat so that it is all well combined and then work in the diced tomatoes. Divide the meat mixture loosely into 12 equal-sized balls.

When you are ready to cook, prepare your barbecue for direct heat cooking (see page 10). I use a plancha for burgers, but a good heavy-based frying pan will work fine too. Heat the pan or plancha until sizzling hot and add the oil. Place the chapli balls on the hot surface and smash them down using a burger press or suitable metal spatula. Placing a piece of greaseproof paper between the burger and the smasher will make this easier. Allow to cook for about 2 minutes before carefully flipping over. Place a piece of cheese on each patty and cover with a burger dome or just let the cheese melt naturally.

To finish, spread green chutney liberally (or to taste) over each bun half. Top the bottom buns with lettuce leaves and sliced tomato and onion. (Feel free to add any other toppings you like too.) Stack the cheese-topped patties on top of each other to make double burgers and then add the stacked burgers to each bun. Cover with the top bun and serve.

PERI-PERI CHICKEN BURGER
SERVES 4

When the Portuguese invaded Goa they brought with them a recipe for peri-peri sauce. The Goans loved it and experimented with the idea, later developing the recipe to become the green Goan cafreal (see page 14), made using green chillies, coriander and mint. Peri-peri is of course now hugely popular all over the world. I featured a recipe for peri-peri chicken in *The Curry Guy Easy*, but here I have tweaked it and put it all on a burger. What could be wrong with that?

PREP TIME: 25 MINS, PLUS
MARINATING TIME
COOKING TIME: 15 MINS

90ml (generous ⅓ cup) rapeseed (canola) oil, plus extra for brushing
1 red onion, roughly chopped
1 large red (bell) pepper, chopped
8 garlic cloves, roughly chopped
4 red bird's eye chillies, roughly chopped
2 tbsp paprika (smoked or unsmoked)
1 tbsp Kashmiri chilli powder
1 tsp ground black pepper
1 tbsp dried red chilli flakes
3 tbsp lime juice
70ml (¼ cup) white wine vinegar
4 large skinless chicken breasts
Salt, to taste

TO SERVE
Approx. 2 tbsp butter
4 burger buns
125ml (½ cup) mayonnaise
Iceberg lettuce leaves
Sliced onion
Sliced tomato
Pickled jalapeño slices
8 slices of burger cheese (optional)

Heat the oil in a frying pan over a medium-high heat and when visibly hot, add the chopped onion and red (bell) pepper. Fry for about 5 minutes, or until the onion is soft and translucent. Add the garlic and chillies and fry for a further minute or so. Stir in 1 tablespoon of the paprika, the chilli powder, black pepper and chilli flakes, ensuring the vegetables are well coated with the spices.

Pour in the lime juice and vinegar and simmer for about 5 minutes to thicken slightly. Allow to cool and then transfer to a blender or food processor and blend to a smooth paste. Season the chicken breasts with salt and the remaining paprika and then cover with about half of the marinade. Cover and leave to marinate in the fridge for about 1 hour or overnight. The longer the better! Remove from the fridge at least 30 minutes before cooking.

When ready to cook, prepare a multi-level direct heat fire (see page 10). Your coals are ready when they turn white-hot and it is uncomfortable to hold your hand 5cm (2in) above the grill for more than 2 seconds.

Butter each of the buns generously and place them on the grill to toast to your liking. Transfer to a plate. Lightly brush the cooking grill with a little oil and place the chicken on the grill over the hottest part of the fire. Cook for about 5 minutes, or until the chicken is about half cooked, then turn to cook the other side. The chicken is done when it reaches an internal temperature of 75°C (165°F). Transfer to the cooler side of the cooking grate while you stack the burgers.

Mix 3 tablespoons of the reserved marinade with the mayonnaise and spread it equally on the bottom buns. Top with the lettuce, onion and tomato and then place a cooked chicken breast on top of each. Add a few pickled jalapeño slices to taste and then cover with a slice of burger cheese and more reserved marinade, if you like. Cover with the top bun and serve.

Left: My chicken mac burger (page 130)
Right: Peri-peri chicken burger

MY CHICKEN MAC BURGER
SERVES 4

Once while in India, I had the sudden urge to try an Indian McDonald's. I knew that beef burgers weren't on the menu in India, so I wanted to see what was on offer. I'm not generally a fan of the burger chain but curiosity overcame me, and my wife and I found ourselves that afternoon trying the Chicken Maharaja Mac. We weren't disappointed! In fact, I liked it so much that I decided to try to recreate it at home, but with grilled chicken burgers instead of fried. Over time the recipe changed until it didn't taste or look much like a Maharaja Mac at all but I liked it so here it is. Enjoy!

PREP TIME: 30 MINS
COOKING TIME: 30 MINS

500g (1lb 2oz) minced (ground) chicken
3 tbsp lamb or beef dripping, softened to room temperature
2 tsp garlic and ginger paste (see page 169)
1 tsp salt
1 tsp freshly ground black pepper

FOR THE SAUCE
6 tbsp mayonnaise
2 tbsp ketchup
1 tbsp American yellow mustard
2 tsp white wine vinegar
15 pickled jalapeños, finely chopped
2 tbsp hot sauce (I use Frank's RedHot brand or my own recipe on page 162)

TO SERVE
4 slices of burger cheese
4 sesame burger buns, plus 4 extra bottom buns for the middles
Approx. 3 tbsp butter
Shredded iceberg lettuce
Thinly sliced red onion
Sliced tomato
16 pickled jalapeño slices

First make the sauce. Mix together all the ingredients in a small bowl until well combined. Refrigerate until needed.

Put the chicken, dripping, garlic and ginger paste, salt and pepper into a bowl and mix well with your hands to combine. Form the mixture into 8 equal-sized flat patties that are slightly larger than the circumference of the buns you are using.

Prepare a direct heat fire (see page 10). When the coals are white-hot and it is uncomfortable to hold your hand 5cm (2in) above the grill for more than 2 seconds, you're ready to cook. Place the patties either directly onto the lightly greased cooking grate or into a frying pan on the grate over direct heat; cook for about 2 minutes, then flip them over. Continue cooking until cooked through and lightly browned and then top 4 of the patties with cheese to melt. Keep warm.

To build the burgers, generously spread the burger sauce over the bottom and middle buns. Place shredded lettuce and sliced onion on top of the sauce, then place the sliced tomato and jalapeños on the middle bun. Top each bun with a cooked chicken burger, then stack the burgers and finish with the top bun.

BRITISH INDIAN RESTAURANT-STYLE CURRIES

British Indian restaurant-style (BIR) curries are perfect cooked on the barbecue. Not only can you precook the meat and vegetables right over a direct heat fire, you can do it before or while you're cooking up the different sauces. Another bonus is that you can achieve much higher cooking temperatures than you can on your kitchen hob, closer to the heat these recipes are cooked over in restaurants. This helps achieve the important caramelization that adds so much to the flavour.

In this section I have included some of the most popular BIR curries. These recipes are all for curry-house portions that serve 1–2 people.

DECIDING WHAT TO COOK

The beauty of this chapter is that you can prepare a couple of sauces (or more!) and then just add whatever cooked meats or vegetables you like, right off the skewer or grill. The tandoori chicken used in the butter chicken on page 102 will work really well for these sauces, as will lamb tikka marinated in the burra kebab marinade on page 21, or the simple namak mandi kebabs on page 44. You can also get creative and use one or more of the other grilled meat and vegetable recipes. Try one of these sauces with chunks of seekh kebabs (meat or vegetarian) – so good!

GETTING YOUR INGREDIENTS READY

Before cooking any curry, it's a good idea to get all your ingredients ready, but this is especially true for BIR curries, which are cooked fast. You don't want to be running around looking for ingredients when you've got your coals to the perfect heat, after all. I cook these BIR curries on my barbecue all the time and when I've got friends around, I like to take requests.

One simple way to do this is to bottle up the dried spice ingredients for the different curries. Doing this will make it easy for you to take orders from hungry friends and you'll know what goes into the different curries without needing to check a recipe. I tend not to include the chilli powder in these blends, adding it to taste instead, to avoid cooking curries that are too spicy for friends that don't like too much heat.

MAKING MIXED POWDER

To make the 'mixed powder' called for in most of these recipes, mix together 4 tablespoons mild curry powder, 1 tablespoon garam masala and 3 tablespoons each of ground cumin, ground coriander, ground turmeric and paprika. To make more or less, simply scale the recipe up or down following the same ratios. The mixed powder will keep for up to 3 months in a sealed jar. If you can't be bothered to make mixed powder (though I hope you do), just use a good-quality curry powder whenever it is called for.

THE CURRY BASE

There's no way around it... if you want to make authentic tasting BIR curries, you need to prepare the essential base sauce. The good news is that it is really easy to prepare and now even easier and tastier if you use my ember-cooked curry base opposite. I have also included a more traditional – and quicker – method should you wish to try that (see the Note on the opposite page). The smooth base is what gives BIR curries their famous texture and flavour. It is quite bland in flavour, in the same way that a vegetable or chicken stock is bland before you add other ingredients to it, but it needs to be as it is used in everything from the mildest korma to the spiciest phall. The magic happens when that bland base sauce hits the curry pan with all the different ingredients used to prepare the curries.

EMBER-COOKED CURRY BASE
MAKES 3 LITRES (3 US QUARTS), OR ENOUGH FOR APPROX. 10 CURRIES

One of the biggest complaints I've heard over the years since starting my blog is that you have to make the base sauce before starting to cook a typical curry-house curry. However, it only takes about an hour to do and most of the work is passive cooking, so it really isn't a lot of fuss. You wouldn't find the following method in any restaurants, but it works so well! Here, the vegetables are all cooked in the embers, so you can do it even if you aren't preparing curries on your barbecue. This is my favourite base for BIR curries.

PREP TIME: 15 MINS
COOKING TIME: 1 HOUR

4 large onions, unpeeled
½ carrot, thinly sliced
½ yellow (bell) pepper, thinly sliced
½ red (bell) pepper, thinly sliced
3 tomatoes, quartered
15 garlic cloves, unpeeled
5cm (2in) piece of ginger, peeled and thinly sliced
125ml (½ cup) rapeseed (canola) oil or melted ghee
½ tsp salt
1 tbsp paprika
1 tbsp ground cumin
1 tbsp ground coriander
1 tbsp garam masala (see page 168)
1 tsp ground turmeric
1 tbsp dried fenugreek leaves (kasoori methi)

Prepare a direct heat fire (see page 10). When the coals have ashed over and are really hot, place the whole, unpeeled onions directly onto the coals. Cook for 40–60 minutes, turning from time to time. The onions are ready when they are totally black on the exterior and so soft you can stick a fork in without any resistance.

Meanwhile, place the remaining vegetables on a large piece of foil along with the garlic and ginger, toss with half of the oil or melted ghee and sprinkle with the salt. Wrap tightly with the foil and then wrap again with two more layers of foil. Place the vegetable parcel right down in the embers with the onions. It is important that you watch this and extinguish any large flames as these will penetrate the parcel and burn the vegetables. Cook for about 40 minutes, or until soft. Feel free to cook other things on the barbecue while the onions and vegetables are cooking.

When the onions and vegetables are soft and cooked through, remove them from the embers and leave to rest until cool enough to handle. Remove the onion skins and roughly chop the flesh. I like a bit of smoky char in my sauce, but you can always wash the cooked onions if you don't. Pour the remaining oil into a large saucepan and add the cooked onions and vegetables along with the ground spices and dried fenugreek leaves (kasoori methi) and stir well. Add 1 litre (4 cups) water and bring to a rolling simmer. Blend with a stick blender until smooth. It will probably still be quite thick. To add to your curries, it will need to be the consistency of full-fat (whole) milk, so add more water as required. This sauce will keep in the fridge for about 3 days, or it can be frozen in small portions for 6 months.

NOTE
I really hope you try this recipe as is, but if you want to make this the more traditional way, roughly chop and fry the onions in 125ml (½ cup) rapeseed (canola) oil for 2 minutes. Add the remaining ingredients, cover with water and simmer for about 1 hour until soft. Blend until smooth, diluting with more water or stock as above.

TIKKA MASALA SAUCE

SERVES 1–2

Tandoori chicken tikka is of course the most popular addition to this sauce, but you're not limited to that, so grill up your favourite main ingredient and add it to this hugely popular, world-famous curry.

PREP TIME: 10 MINS
COOKING TIME: 10 MINS

2 tbsp rapeseed (canola) oil or ghee
1 tbsp garlic and ginger paste (see page 169)
1 tbsp mixed powder (see page 132)
1 tbsp tandoori masala (see page 167)
1 tsp paprika
1 tsp sugar (more or less to taste)
1 tbsp ground almonds
1 tbsp coconut flour or coconut milk powder
4 tbsp tomato purée (see page 169)
Approx. 300ml (1¼ cups) curry base (see page 133), heated
70ml (¼ cup) single (light) cream
3 tbsp finely chopped coriander (cilantro)
1 tbsp cold butter
Juice of ½ lemon
½ tsp garam masala (see page 168)
1 tsp dried fenugreek leaves (kasoori methi)
Salt, to taste

Heat the oil or ghee in a frying pan over a high heat and then stir in the garlic and ginger paste. Fry for about 30 seconds, then add the ground spices, sugar, ground almonds and coconut flour or milk powder. Stir well. The ground spices will become dry and crumbly fast. This is your cue to add the tomato purée. Stir well to form a smooth tikka masala paste.

Next add 1–2 ladles of curry base and stir to combine. Bring to a simmer and let it bubble for about 2 minutes, stirring only if the sauce is sticking to the pan. As the sauce simmers, you will see that it begins to caramelize on the sides of the pan. Stir this in for more amazing flavour. As there are so many vegetables in the base, it will thicken quickly.

Add your meat or vegetables and a little more curry base if needed and simmer until everything is heated through, about 2 minutes. If the curry is looking too dry, add more curry base. If too saucy, just cook it down for a couple of minutes.

Just before serving, stir in the cream, followed by the chopped coriander, butter, lemon juice, garam masala and dried fenugreek leaves (kasoori methi). Taste and season with salt as needed.

Clockwise from top left: Korma sauce (page 136); tikka masala sauce; rezala sauce (page 138)

KORMA SAUCE
SERVES 1–2

Tandoori chicken and paneer are very good options for this sauce. I often add thinly sliced raw chicken and let it cook through in the simmering curry but tandoori chicken will add another layer of flavour.

PREP TIME: 10 MINS
COOKING TIME: 10 MINS

2 tbsp ghee or rapeseed (canola) oil
2.5cm (1in) cinnamon stick
2 green cardamom pods, bruised
1 tsp garlic and ginger paste (see page 169)
1½ tbsp sugar, plus extra to taste
3 tbsp ground almonds
1 tbsp coconut flour or coconut milk powder
300ml (1¼ cups) curry base (see page 133), heated
50g (2oz) creamed coconut
1 tsp garam masala (see page 168)
70ml (¼ cup) single (light) cream
½ tsp rose water
1 tbsp cold butter
Salt, to taste

Heat the ghee or oil in a frying pan over a high heat. When it starts to bubble, toss in the cinnamon and cardamom pods and fry for about 30 seconds, then stir in the garlic and ginger paste. Fry for about 20 seconds before adding the sugar, ground almonds and coconut flour or coconut milk powder. Stir well, then add 1–2 ladles of base sauce and allow to bubble.

Break up the creamed coconut and add it to the simmering sauce. Add a splash more curry base from time to time as the curry simmers, only stirring if the sauce is sticking to the sides of the pan. Add your meat or vegetables. If using raw chicken as suggested above, press it right into the sauce so that it cooks quickly and evenly. Swirl in the garam masala.

When the meat or vegetables are cooked or heated through, remove the cardamom pods and cinnamon stick and stir in the cream.

Add the rose water and finish with the butter. Season with salt and more sugar to taste.

JALFREZI SAUCE
SERVES 1–2

Unlike other British Indian curries, in which precooked meat is used for speed, jalfrezis have always been made with precooked meat. This is a spicy stir fry, with the only real difference between the curry-house jalfrezi and the Indian version being the base sauce – and perhaps the chefs' slightly different spice blend.

PREP TIME: 10 MINS
COOKING TIME: 10 MINS

2 tbsp vegetable oil
½ tsp black mustard seeds
5 fresh or frozen curry leaves (optional)
1 onion, thinly sliced
½ red (bell) pepper, thinly sliced
¼ green (bell) pepper, thinly sliced
1 tbsp garlic and ginger paste (see page 169)
2–3 green bird's eye chillies, finely chopped
½ tsp Kashmiri chilli powder
1 tbsp mixed powder (see page 132)
2 tbsp tomato purée (see page 169)
250ml (1 cup) curry base (see page 133), heated
Salt, to taste
1 small bunch of coriander (cilantro), leaves chopped

Heat the oil in a frying pan over a high heat. When hot, add the mustard seeds. When they begin to crackle, stir in the curry leaves. Fry for about 20 seconds to infuse the flavours into the oil.

Next add the onion and (bell) peppers and fry for about 3 minutes. You want the vegetables to be starting to soften, but still have a bit of crunch. Stir in the garlic and ginger paste and fry for a further 30 seconds and then stir in the green chillies, chilli powder and mixed powder.

Add the tomato purée and 1–2 ladles of curry base. Let this come to a simmer for a couple of minutes. Do not stir unless the sauce is sticking to the pan. Add your meat or vegetables and a splash more curry base to thin if necessary. Cook it down to your preferred consistency, season with salt and garnish with the chopped coriander (cilantro).

CHASNI SAUCE
SERVES 1–2

Although chicken tikka masala and jalfrezi are without a doubt the most popular curry-house curries, chasni is up-and-coming and might just surpass them one day. This is a delicious sweet-and-sour curry sauce that tastes even better when cooked over fire. It is usually bright red due to the addition of red food colouring but I usually leave it out.

PREP TIME: 10 MINS
COOKING TIME: 10 MINS

2 tbsp rapeseed (canola) oil
1 tbsp garlic and ginger paste (see page 169)
¼ tsp ground turmeric
1 generous tsp ground cumin
300ml (1¼ cups) curry base (see page 133), heated
1½ tbsp mango chutney
1 tbsp mint sauce (see page 161, or use shop-bought)
2 tbsp ketchup
70ml (¼ cup) single (light) cream
¼ tsp garam masala (see page 168)
Salt, to taste
1½ tbsp finely chopped coriander (cilantro)

Heat the oil in a frying pan over a high heat. When hot, stir in the garlic and ginger paste and fry for about 30 seconds. Stir in the turmeric and cumin and then add about half the base sauce. Bring this to a rolling simmer, stirring only if the sauce is sticking to the pan.

Add your meat or vegetables, along with the mango chutney, mint sauce and ketchup and bring to a simmer, gradually adding the remaining curry base.

When the sauce has cooked down to your preferred consistency, swirl in the cream. To finish, stir in the garam masala, season with salt and garnish with the coriander (cilantro).

PATHIA SAUCE
SERVES 1–2

Like the chasni opposite, pathia curries are well known for their sweet-and-sour flavour. Pathias are a little spicier, but you could of course adjust this to taste by adding more or less chilli powder. I usually go for more, but then I like my curries hot!

PREP TIME: 10 MINS
COOKING TIME: 10 MINS

2 tbsp rapeseed (canola) oil
½ onion, finely chopped
1 tbsp garlic and ginger paste (see page 169)
1 tbsp mango chutney
½ tsp tamarind paste
1 tbsp mixed powder (see page 132)
½ tsp Kashmiri chilli powder
1 tbsp sugar
70ml (¼ cup) tomato purée (see page 169)
300ml (1¼ cups) curry base (see page 133), heated
½ tsp dried fenugreek leaves (kasoori methi)
Salt, to taste
Juice of ½ lemon
2 tbsp finely chopped coriander (cilantro), to serve

Heat the oil in a frying pan over a high heat. When hot, add the chopped onion and fry for about 3 minutes, or until soft and translucent. Stir in the garlic and ginger paste and fry for a further 30 seconds, then add mango chutney and tamarind paste, followed by the mixed powder, chilli powder and sugar. Give this all a good stir and then add the tomato purée. Bring to a simmer and then add half the curry base. Simmer, only stirring if the sauce is sticking to the pan. The sauce will begin to caramelize on the sides of the pan – scrape this back into the sauce.

Add your meat or vegetables along with the remaining curry base and bring to a simmer. Continue simmering for a few minutes until you are happy with the consistency.

Add the dried fenugreek leaves (kasoori methi) by rubbing the leaves between your fingers. Season with salt and finish with a good squeeze of lemon and the coriander (cilantro).

REZALA SAUCE
SERVES 1–2

Rezala sauce is so good; whenever I have a curry barbecue at my place it's probably the most requested. Rezala curries are often quite red in colour but they can also be creamy as in the photo on page 135. If you like a redder sauce, just increase the amount of puréed tomatoes and/or chilli powder.

PREP TIME: 10 MINS
COOKING TIME: 10 MINS

2 tbsp rapeseed (canola) oil
½ onion, finely chopped
1 tbsp garlic and ginger paste (see page 169)
2 green bird's eye chillies, chopped
1 tbsp mixed powder (see page 132)
1 tsp Kashmiri chilli powder (or more or less to taste)
3 tbsp tomato purée (see page 169)
300ml (1¼ cups) curry base (see page 133), heated
70ml (¼ cup) single (light) cream, or to taste
1 tbsp cold butter
½ tsp garam masala (see page 168)
Salt, to taste
2 tbsp finely chopped coriander (cilantro)

Heat the oil in a frying pan over direct high heat until visibly hot. Stir in the chopped onion and add a pinch of salt. Fry, stirring regularly for about 3 minutes, or until soft and translucent. Add the garlic and ginger paste and chopped chillies and fry for a further 30 seconds before stirring in the mixed powder and chilli powder.

Add the tomato purée followed by 1–2 ladles of the curry base. Bring this to a bubbling simmer, only stirring if the sauce is sticking to the sides of the pan.

After about 2 minutes, add your meat or vegetables to the simmering sauce. Be sure to top it up with more base from time to time if the curry is looking dry; if you add too much, just cook it down until you are happy with the consistency.

Once your main ingredient is heated through, swirl in the cream. Add the butter to melt into the sauce. Season with salt and sprinkle with the garam masala. Garnish with coriander (cilantro).

CHILLI-GARLIC SAUCE
SERVES 1–2

This spicy sauce is one of my all-time favourites. I've kept the heat down so everyone can try this, but if you like your curries really hot, go ahead and add more chillies and/or chilli powder.

PREP TIME: 10 MINS
COOKING TIME: 10 MINS

2 tbsp rapeseed (canola) oil
8 garlic cloves, thinly sliced
½ onion, finely chopped
1 tbsp garlic and ginger paste (see page 169)
2 green bird's eye chillies, thinly sliced
½ tsp Kashmiri chilli powder
1 tbsp mixed powder (see page 132)
1 tbsp tandoori masala (see page 167)
70ml (¼ cup) tomato purée (see page 169)
300ml (1¼ cups) curry base (see page 133), heated
½ tsp dried fenugreek leaves (kasoori methi)
Salt, to taste
2 tbsp finely chopped coriander (cilantro)

Heat the oil in a frying pan over a high heat. When hot, add the garlic. Fry for about 2 minutes, being very careful not to burn the garlic. Add the onion and a pinch of salt and fry for 2 minutes more, then stir in the garlic and ginger paste and the chillies. Continue cooking for about 20 seconds, then add the ground spices and tomato purée. Stir this into a thick paste and then add about half the curry base. Bring to a simmer and cook, only stirring if the sauce is obviously sticking to the pan.

Add your meat or vegetables and continue to simmer. As the sauce simmers, you will notice that it caramelizes around the edges of the pan. Scrape this into the sauce. Add the remaining curry base and simmer until you are happy with the consistency of the sauce.

To finish, add the dried fenugreek leaves (kasoori methi) by rubbing them between your fingers. Season with salt to taste and garnish with the coriander (cilantro).

BHUNA SAUCE
SERVES 1–2

Curry-house-style bhuna curries may not be much like traditional bhunas, but they do have one thing in common and that is they aren't very saucy. If you're keen to cook up a few naans over the fire, this is a great recipe to serve them with. No need for cutlery! Just scoop the curry up with naans or chapatis.

PREP TIME: 10 MINS
COOKING TIME: 10 MINS

2 tbsp ghee or rapeseed (canola) oil
½ onion, finely chopped
¼ red (bell) pepper, diced
1 tbsp garlic and ginger paste (see page 169)
2 tbsp finely chopped coriander (cilantro) stalks
70ml (¼ cup) tomato purée (see page 169)
1 tbsp mixed powder (see page 132)
1 tbsp tandoori masala (see page 167)
250ml (1 cup) curry base (see page 133), heated
1 tbsp natural yoghurt
2 tbsp finely chopped coriander (cilantro)
Juice of 1 lime
1 red spur chilli, thinly sliced
Salt, to taste

Heat the ghee or oil in a frying pan over a high heat. When hot, add the chopped onion and (bell) pepper and fry for about 4 minutes, or until the onion is soft and translucent. Stir in the garlic and ginger paste along with the coriander (cilantro) stalks and fry for a further 30 seconds.

Stir in the tomato purée and when it begins to simmer, stir in the mixed powder and tandoori masala, followed by about half the curry base. Bring this to a simmer and let it bubble for a couple of minutes, only stirring if the sauce is sticking to the pan.

Add your precooked meat or vegetables, then add the remaining curry base and continue simmering until you have a really thick sauce. The sauce should be sticking to your main ingredients.

Stir in the yoghurt and check for seasoning, adding salt to taste. Top with the coriander, a good squeeze of lime juice and the sliced chilli.

DHANSAK SAUCE
SERVES 1–2

Many curry-house dhansaks, especially in the north, have pineapple in them. Though pineapple chunks are not always included, pineapple juice is almost always added for flavour. I tend to leave out the chunks but it's completely up to you.

PREP TIME: 10 MINS
COOKING TIME: 10 MINS

2 tbsp rapeseed (canola) oil
1 tbsp garlic and ginger paste (see page 169)
½ tsp ground turmeric
1 tbsp mixed powder (see page 132)
½ tsp Kashmiri chilli powder
70ml (¼ cup) tomato purée (see page 169)
250ml (1 cup) curry base (see page 133), heated
60ml (scant ¼ cup) pineapple juice (or use stock or more base sauce)
90g (scant ½ cup) cooked red lentils
3 tinned (canned) pineapple rings, cut into cubes (optional)
Juice of 1 lemon
Salt, to taste
1 tbsp finely chopped coriander (cilantro)

Heat the oil in a frying pan over a direct high heat. When hot, add the garlic and ginger paste and fry for about 30 seconds. Stir in the turmeric, mixed powder and chilli powder.

Add the tomato purée and cook briefly, then add about half the curry base and bring to a simmer. Only stir if the sauce looks like it is sticking to the pan.

Add your precooked meat or vegetables, then stir in the remaining curry base and the pineapple juice along with the cooked lentils and continue to simmer, being careful not to burn the lentils. If the sauce is looking dry, add more base sauce. To finish, stir in the pineapples chunks, if using, and lemon juice. Season with salt and garnish with the coriander (cilantro).

SAAG SAUCE
SERVES 1–2

This saag curry sauce is so good with just about everything. Try it with cubed paneer – the aged mango paneer recipe on page 87 is a good one here, although raw, cubed paneer added and heated through just before serving is also delicious. Tandoori chicken or lamb tikka is also amazing. If you're a saag fan like I am, you really can't go wrong.

PREP TIME: 10 MINS
COOKING TIME: 10 MINS

110g (4oz) baby spinach leaves
3 green bird's eye chillies, roughly chopped
Handful of coriander (cilantro) leaves, plus 1 tbsp finely chopped coriander stalks
Juice of 1 lime, plus lime wedges to serve
2 tbsp ghee or rapeseed (canola) oil
½ onion, finely chopped
1½ tbsp garlic and ginger paste (see page 169)
1 tsp ground cumin
1 tsp ground coriander
2 tbsp mixed powder (see page 132)
½ tsp Kashmiri chilli powder
70ml (¼ cup) tomato purée (see page 169)
250ml (1 cup) curry base (see page 133), heated
1 tbsp natural yoghurt
½ tsp garam masala (see page 168)
Salt, to taste

Put the spinach, chillies, coriander (cilantro) leaves and lime juice into a food processor and blend to a smooth paste, adding a little water if necessary. Set aside.

Heat the ghee or oil in a wok or large frying pan over a high, direct heat. When hot, add the chopped onion and fry for about 5 minutes, or until translucent and soft but not overly browned. Add the ginger and garlic paste and coriander stalks and sizzle for about 30 seconds. Add the ground cumin, ground coriander, mixed powder and chilli powder and stir to combine, then add the tomato purée to the pan, followed by 1–2 ladles of the curry base.

Bring this to a simmer and allow to bubble for about 3 minutes, only stirring if the sauce is sticking to the pan. Top up with more curry base from time to time if the sauce is too dry. Next, add the blended spinach mixture and cook for a further 2 minutes to thicken slightly. It will darken a little as it simmers.

Add your precooked meat, vegetables or paneer and heat them through in the sauce. You can always add more curry sauce if needed. Check for seasoning and add salt to taste. Just before serving stir in the yoghurt and sprinkle over the garam masala. Serve with lime wedges for squeezing over.

Clockwise from top left: Saag sauce (with paneer); chasni sauce (page 137); rogan josh sauce (page 142)

ROGAN JOSH SAUCE
SERVES 1–2

I prefer rogan josh with lamb. However, chicken, prawns (shrimp) or vegetables are also good options. The cashew paste for this recipe can be made by blending 10 cashew nuts with just enough water to make a paste.

PREP TIME: 10 MINS
COOKING TIME: 10 MINS

2 tbsp rapeseed (canola) oil or ghee
1 tbsp garlic and ginger paste (see page 169)
1–2 tbsp paprika
1½ tsp ground cumin
1 tbsp mixed powder (see page 132)
1 tsp Kashmiri chilli powder (or more or less to taste)
70ml (¼ cup) tomato purée (see page 169)
300ml (1¼ cup) curry base (see page 133), heated
1 generous tbsp cashew paste (see above)
1½ tbsp natural yoghurt
1 tomato, quartered
½ tsp garam masala (see page 168)
1 tsp dried fenugreek leaves (kasoori methi)
Salt, to taste
2 tbsp chopped coriander (cilantro)
Chopped red onion, to serve

Heat the oil or ghee in a frying pan over a direct high heat. When visibly hot, stir in the garlic and ginger paste and let it sizzle for about 30 seconds. Stir in the ground spices.

Add the tomato purée followed by 1–2 ladles of the curry base. Bring to a simmer, then add your precooked meat or vegetables. Simmer for a couple of minutes, adding more curry base as needed, until the sauce reaches your preferred consistency. Only stir if the sauce is sticking to the pan. Stir in the cashew paste and then the yoghurt a teaspoon at a time, whisking as you do to combine. Finally, add the quartered tomato and push it down into the sauce.

Season with salt and the garam masala and add the dried fenugreek leaves by rubbing them between your fingers. Garnish with the coriander (cilantro) and chopped red onion.

MADRAS SAUCE
SERVES 1–2

Do you like a Madras sweet or savoury? The smooth mango chutney used in this recipe gives it a nice, sweet flavour, but it can be substituted with a savoury lime pickle instead.

PREP TIME: 10 MINS
COOKING TIME: 10 MINS

2 tbsp rapeseed (canola) oil
2 dried Kashmiri chillies
2 green cardamom pods
1½ tbsp garlic and ginger paste (see page 169)
2 green bird's eye chillies, finely chopped
2 tsp ground cumin
½ tsp ground coriander
¼ tsp ground turmeric
1 tbsp Kashmiri chilli powder
1 tbsp mixed powder (see page 132)
70ml (¼ cup) tomato purée (see page 169)
300ml (1¼ cups) curry base (see page 133), heated
1 tbsp smooth mango chutney
Juice of ½ lime
Salt, to taste
½ tsp garam masala (see page 168)
1 tbsp chopped coriander (cilantro)

Heat the oil in a frying pan over a direct high heat. Add the Kashmiri chillies and cardamom pods. Move the spices around to flavour the oil for 30 seconds and then add the garlic and ginger paste. Fry for a further 30 seconds.

Add the chopped green chillies, followed by all the ground spices and stir to combine. Add the tomato purée followed by 1–2 ladles of the curry base and bring to a simmer. Allow to bubble for 2–3 minutes, stirring only if the sauce is sticking to the pan.

Add your precooked meat or vegetables and the remaining curry base and let it all simmer for a couple of minutes. Next, stir in the mango chutney and lime juice. Simmer for a further 2 minutes, only stirring if the sauce is obviously sticking to the pan.

Season with salt, sprinkle with the garam masala and garnish with the coriander (cilantro).

VINDALOO SAUCE
SERVES 1–2

If you like a good vindaloo, this recipe will get you the results you're looking for. It's spicy, but not so spicy you can't enjoy the other flavours.

PREP TIME: 10 MINS
COOKING TIME: 10 MINS

2 tbsp rapeseed (canola) oil
3 green cardamom pods, bruised
1 star anise
1 Indian bay leaf
1 tbsp garlic and ginger paste (see page 169)
2 green bird's eye chillies, finely chopped
1 scotch bonnet chilli, finely chopped
½ tsp ground turmeric
1 tbsp Kashmiri chilli powder
1 tbsp mixed powder (see page 132)
70ml (¼ cup) tomato purée (see page 169)
300ml (1¼ cups) curry base (see page 133), heated
1 tbsp white wine vinegar
½ tsp dried fenugreek leaves (kasoori methi)
1 large cooked potato, peeled and cut into 6 pieces
Salt, to taste
1 tbsp finely chopped coriander (cilantro)

Heat the oil in a frying pan over a high direct heat and then throw in the cardamom pods, star anise and bay leaf. Let the whole spices infuse into the oil for about 30 seconds, then stir in the garlic and ginger paste. Add the green and scotch bonnet chillies and fry for about 30 seconds, then add the ground spices and fry for a further 30 seconds.

Your pan might be looking a bit dry at this point, so add the tomato purée and about half the curry base and bring to a simmer. Only stir if it looks like the sauce is sticking to the pan. Add your precooked meat or vegetables and the remaining curry base. If the curry is looking dry, just add more base sauce; if it's too saucy, just cook it down for a couple of minutes.

Once you are happy with the consistency, add the vinegar and then the fenugreek leaves by rubbing them between your fingers. Finally, add the cooked potato and season with salt. Finish with the chopped coriander (cilantro).

PHAAL SAUCE
SERVES 1–2

How hot you make your phaal curries is really up to you. I think this is a good spicy blend but feel free to adjust the heat!

PREP TIME: 10 MINS
COOKING TIME: 10 MINS

2 tbsp rapeseed (canola) oil or mustard oil
½ small onion, finely chopped
4 habanero chillies, finely chopped
3 green bird's eye chillies, finely chopped
1 tbsp garlic and ginger paste (see page 169)
1 tbsp mixed powder (see page 132)
1 tbsp Kashmiri chilli powder
70ml (¼ cup) tomato purée (see page 169)
300ml (1¼ cups) curry base (see page 133), heated
1 tbsp naga pickle (optional; I use Mr Naga brand)
1 tsp dried fenugreek leaves (kasoori methi)
1 tbsp julienned ginger
1 tbsp finely chopped coriander (cilantro)

Heat the oil in a large frying pan over a direct high heat. Add the chopped onion and fry for 5 minutes, or until soft and translucent. Stir in the habanero chillies and bird's eye chillies followed by the garlic and ginger paste and fry for about 30 seconds. Add the mixed powder and Kashmiri chilli powder followed by the tomato purée and stir to combine, then add about 125ml (½ cup) of the curry base.

Bring to a simmer and add your meat or vegetables. Add the remaining curry base, return to a simmer and bubble for a couple of minutes, only stirring if the sauce is sticking to the pan. As you cook, the sauce will caramelize on the sides of the pan – stir this in as it adds flavour.

Stir in the naga pickle, if using, and continue to simmer the curry until you are happy with the consistency. Season with salt and sprinkle the dried fenugreek leaves (kasoori methi) over the top by rubbing them between your fingers.

Finish with the julienned ginger and chopped coriander (cilantro).

SIDES

From delicious smoky dhal to a selection of my favourite rice and Indian bread recipes, you'll find it all here – and they are all so good cooked over fire. If you like chips with your curry, be sure to try the masala garlic fries too!

This section demonstrates so much of what can be done cooked over fire. Grilling, roasting, boiling and deep-frying… all can be done and I hope you enjoy firing up your barbecue to do just that.

SMOKED CHANA DHAL
SERVES 6

The smoky, creamy dhal found at many of the street-food stalls in India is to die for! This is my version. The recipe uses a technique called dhungar, which smokes food without needing a barbecue – though it is a lot more convenient if you have a charcoal fire burning. The dhungar method can be used for all sorts of things – it's ideal for making smoky tandoori chicken in a conventional oven.

PREP TIME: 15 MINS, PLUS SOAKING TIME
COOKING TIME: 1 HOUR 15 MINS, PLUS SMOKING TIME

400g (2 cups) chana dhal, rinsed and soaked for 30–60 minutes (see Notes)
1 tbsp plus 1 tsp melted ghee
½ red onion, finely chopped
2 tbsp garlic and ginger paste (see page 169)
3 green bird's eye chillies, finely chopped
1 tomato, diced
1 tsp ground cumin
1 tbsp ground coriander
½ tsp ground turmeric
1 tbsp Kashmiri chilli powder (more or less to taste)
Salt, to taste

FOR THE TARKA
3 tbsp ghee
3 dried Kashmiri chillies
½ tsp asafoetida (see Notes)
1 tsp cumin seeds
2 garlic cloves, thinly sliced

Prepare a direct heat lumpwood charcoal fire (see pages 9–10). When it is uncomfortable to hold your hand 5cm (2in) above the grill for more than 2 seconds, the fire is ready.

Bring 500ml (2 cups) water to a boil in a saucepan and then add the soaked chana dhal. Simmer, uncovered, for 45–60 minutes, or until the lentils are soft and creamy. Keep an eye on the lentils and skim off any foam that rises to the top, stir them regularly to make sure they don't stick to the bottom of the pan, and top up with more water if needed.

Meanwhile, heat 1 tablespoon of the ghee in a saucepan or karahi over the hot fire next to the simmering lentils. When bubbling hot, add the chopped onion and fry for about 5 minutes, or until soft and translucent. Stir in the garlic and ginger paste and chopped chillies and fry for a further 30 seconds and then add the diced tomato and ground spices. This is your base masala. Remove from the heat and set aside.

Once the lentils have cooked, remove from the heat. Take a small piece of lumpwood charcoal and place it in a small metal dish or on a piece of foil. Make a small well in the cooked lentils and place the dish or foil and burning charcoal in it. Drizzle the charcoal with the remaining melted ghee to make it smoke and cover the pan. Leave for 20–30 minutes, or until the smoke has almost died off.

Remove the charcoal from the lentils and return the base masala to the heat. Pour in the cooked lentils and stir well to combine. Taste and season with salt.

Heat the ghee for the tarka in a small frying pan. When hot, add the other ingredients and fry for about 1 minute, or until the garlic is soft. Pour the tarka over the dhal to serve.

NOTES
You could substitute masoor dhal (red lentils), which will cook in half the time. You may also prefer to cook the dhal indoors and take it outside, ready to smoke and finish off on the fire.

If you are gluten-free, please check the asafoetida packaging as some brands contain wheat flour.

MASALA GARLIC FRIES
SERVES 4-6

I'm a big fan of frozen chips (fries). I've prepared homemade, hand-cut chips on numerous occasions but find it to be a lot of work with little real benefit. Frozen chips are what are used at most of the best burger joints and takeaways, so they are good enough for me when cooking at home, too. When making homemade chips, you need to fry them twice or even three times. Frozen chips have already been fried once so all you need to do is give them that last fry for a perfect result. These are a delicious side accompaniment to German currywurst (see page 72). You will find a photograph of them on that page too.

PREP TIME: 10 MINS
COOKING TIME: 10-15 MINS

Rapeseed (canola) oil, for
   deep-frying
900g (2lb) frozen chips (fries)
   for frying (not oven chips)
1 red onion, thinly sliced
8 green chillies, thinly sliced
   lengthways
3 tbsp ghee
8 large garlic cloves, smashed
   and roughly chopped
1 generous tbsp Kashmiri chilli
   powder
1 tsp chaat masala (optional; see
   page 168)
3 tbsp finely chopped coriander
   (cilantro)
Salt, to taste

Half-fill a flat-bottomed wok or saucepan with oil and bring up to 180°C (355°F) but if the instruction on the bag of chips (fries) you have suggests a different cooking temperature, go with that instead. You will probably need to fry in batches as you don't want to overcrowd the pan or the oil will cool down and you'll end up with limp, oily fries. Fry the chips for 2 minutes per batch, or until crispy. Transfer to paper towels to soak up any excess oil.

When cooking the last batch of fries, add the sliced onion and chillies and fry those too.

Heat the ghee in a frying pan over a high heat and fry the garlic until golden. Be careful not to burn it. You want a light brown exterior and soft centre, which should only take a minute or so.

Place the hot fries, onion and chillies in a serving bowl and toss with the Kashmiri chilli powder, chaat masala, if using, and salt to taste. Pour the garlic and ghee over the top and mix well, then sprinkle with the coriander before serving.

BASMATI RICE TWO WAYS
SERVES 2

PREP TIME: 3 MINS, PLUS SOAKING TIME
COOKING TIME: 8–40 MINS, DEPENDING ON METHOD USED

Both of these methods make excellent, fluffy basmati rice. I prefer the steamed method, but you might prefer the quicker boiled version. These recipes make two servings, but they can be scaled up by simply doubling, tripling or quadrupling the amount of rice and adjusting the amount of water accordingly.

STEAMING METHOD

185g (1 cup) basmati rice
½ tsp salt
70ml (¼ cup) melted ghee (optional)

Put the rice into a bowl and cover with cold water. Swirl the water; it will become milky from the rice starch. Pour the water out and add fresh water. Repeat until the water is almost clear – you will need to do this several times. Cover with water once more and leave to soak for 30–60 minutes.

Drain the rice and transfer to a saucepan with a tight-fitting lid. Cover with 375ml (1½ cups) water and add the salt. Place the covered pan over a high heat and bring to a boil. When it boils, remove from the heat and allow to steam without removing the lid for 40 minutes. Lift the lid and carefully fluff the cooked rice with a fork. Do not stir too rigorously or the grains will split and become mushy. Serve as is or drizzled with the melted ghee.

NOTE
When steaming rice in this way, the rice to water ratio is always 1 part rice to 1½ parts water. For best results, never fill your pan more than one-third full with the rice and water.

BOILING METHOD

185g (1 cup) basmati rice
½ tsp salt
70ml (¼ cup) melted ghee (optional)

Put the rice into a bowl and cover with cold water. Swirl the water; it will become milky from the rice starch. Pour the water out and add fresh water. Repeat until the water is almost clear – you will need to do this several times. Cover with water once more and leave to soak for 30–60 minutes.

Bring 1 litre (4 cups) water to a boil in a saucepan and add the salt. Drain the soaked rice, then add to the pan and cook for 6–7 minutes, or until cooked. Strain well through a sieve. Serve as is or drizzled with the melted ghee.

NOTE
To scale up this recipe, you will just need enough water to cover the rice. Even if I triple the recipe, I usually only need about 2 litres (8 cups) water.

ROASTED VEGETABLE FRIED RICE
SERVES 6-8

Although this recipe could be made in one go, I suggest preparing the rice earlier as it needs to cool before it is fried. This makes it a great way to use up leftover rice. Feel free to use more or less of the suggested vegetables or choose others. There's no way I would leave out those heads of soft, roasted garlic though. This makes a great side dish for grilled meats and fish but it is also really good served as a vegetarian main. You can see this rice photographed next to the chicken ghee roast on page 100.

PREP TIME: 10 MINS
COOKING TIME: 15 MINS

2 tbsp ghee or rapeseed (canola) oil
2.5cm (1in) cinnamon stick
3 green cardamom pods, bruised
20 fresh or frozen curry leaves
2 red onions, finely chopped
2 tbsp garlic and ginger paste (see page 169)
6 green bird's eye chillies
2 tomatoes, diced
1 tsp ground cumin
1 tsp Kashmiri chilli powder
½ tsp ground turmeric
1 tsp garam masala (see page 168)
Approx. 750g (3 cups) cold cooked basmati rice (see page 147)
Salt and freshly ground black pepper, to taste

FOR THE ROASTED VEGETABLES
1 red (bell) pepper, diced
½ green (bell) pepper, diced
1 large carrot, diced
2 baby aubergines (eggplants), diced
2 shallots, diced
2 small heads of garlic, halved horizontally
70ml (¼ cup) melted ghee, plus extra to serve
½ tsp salt

Start by preparing the roasted vegetables. Put all the vegetables in a bowl and mix with the melted ghee and salt. Pour the vegetables onto a piece of foil large enough to hold them all and wrap tightly. Then wrap with another layer of foil, so that it is double wrapped. This will help to stop the vegetables burning.

Prepare a multi-level direct heat fire (see page 10). When the flames burn down and the coals are red hot, nestle the parcel of vegetables between them. Cook for about 35 minutes, turning once, preferably with a towel to avoid tearing the foil. This can all be done ahead of time or while you're preparing the rice.

To prepare the rice, heat the ghee or oil in a large frying pan or wok on the grill over the fire. When the oil is visibly hot, stir in the whole spices and curry leaves and allow them to infuse into the oil for about 30 seconds. Stir in the chopped onions and fry for about 5 minutes, or until soft and translucent. Add the garlic and ginger paste, whole chillies and diced tomatoes and fry for a further 30 seconds. Stir in the ground spices and then add the cold, cooked rice.

Gently stir the rice to coat with the spices and then add the roasted vegetables, squeezing the soft cloves from the heads of garlic. Add any remaining ghee from the foil parcel and continue stirring until the rice is hot and crispy in places. Season with salt and pepper. Taste and add more melted ghee if you like.

CRISPY SAFFRON RICE
SERVES 4

There was no way I could give you my flattened beef kebab recipe (see page 48) without featuring this crispy saffron rice recipe too. I learned it from an Iranian friend about 30 years ago and only started making it again when I was reminded how good it was on a recent trip to India.

PREP TIME: 30 MINS
COOKING TIME: 30 MINS

370g (2 cups) basmati rice
3 tsp salt
70ml (¼ cup) melted ghee
2 tbsp olive oil
½ tsp saffron, crushed between your fingers
Juice of 1 lemon (optional)

Put the rice into a bowl and cover with cold water. Swirl the water; it will become milky from the rice starch. Pour the water out and add fresh water. Repeat until the water is almost clear. Cover with water once more and leave to soak for 30 minutes.

Bring 2 litres (8 cups) water to a boil in a large, deep non-stick frying pan with a lid and add the salt. Drain the rice, add to the pan and cook, stirring regularly, for 5 minutes, or until the rice is just beginning to soften but is still not fully cooked. Strain, reserving the cooking water.

Place the pan back over a high heat and add 3 tablespoons of the ghee, the olive oil and the saffron. When hot, add about a quarter of the rice and stir it into the ghee and oil. Spread it out so that it covers the bottom of the pan, then pour in the remaining rice without stirring. Cover with a damp tea (dish) towel and place the lid securely on top. Cook for 4 minutes, then lower the heat and cook for a further 15–20 minutes, or until the rice is tender and the bottom is nice and crispy.

Carefully separate the grains with a fork. Don't stir rigorously or the grains will split. If using the lemon juice, squeeze over the top to serve.

5-MINUTE PARATHAS
MAKES 4

Not everyone wants to go to a lot of work kneading paratha dough, or any dough for that matter. If that's you, I've got you covered. You can make these delicious parathas in minutes. What's more, you can also add different ingredients to the batter to make flavoured parathas, such as cumin seeds or crushed coriander seeds. These breads are delicious on their own, dipped into a curry or used as a wrap for seekh or doner kebabs. A non-stick pan is essential – I recommend picking up a non-stick tawa to make things even easier on yourself.

PREP TIME: 2 MINS
COOKING TIME: 10 MINS

250g (2 cups) plain (all-purpose) flour
1 tsp salt
1 tbsp rapeseed (canola) oil
4 tbsp ghee or rapeseed (canola) oil

Sift the flour into a mixing bowl and then whisk in the salt, 750ml (3 cups) water and the tablespoon of rapeseed (canola) oil. This will make a batter that is very similar in consistency to American pancakes. Place a non-stick frying pan on the cooking grate over a high heat. Add 1 tablespoon of the ghee or oil to the pan and swirl it around to coat.

Pour a ladleful of the batter into the centre of the pan and then spread it out in a circular motion with the bottom of the ladle. Fry for 1–2 minutes, or until lightly toasted on the bottom, then flip it over to cook the other side. Keep the cooked parathas warm while you cook the rest.

POTATO PARATHAS
MAKES 4

Although these garlicky potato parathas are delicious served on their own as a starter, they are even better dipped into the roasted onion raita on page 161. Depending on your outdoor setup, you might want to prepare the parathas indoors. Cooking them in a tawa or pan outdoors over the fire is a must though – there are few things better than hot potato parathas served right off the fire.

PREP TIME: 40 MINS
COOKING TIME: 20 MINS

2 tbsp melted ghee, plus extra
    for brushing
1 tsp cumin seeds
6 garlic cloves, finely chopped
10 fresh or frozen curry leaves,
    roughly chopped
3 green bird's eye chillies, finely
    chopped
1 tsp salt
½–1 tsp dried red chilli flakes
    (more or less to taste)
250g (1 cup) fine semolina
2 par-boiled potatoes, finely
    grated
Plain (all-purpose) flour,
    for dusting
1 red onion, finely chopped
    (optional)

Heat the ghee in a frying pan over a high heat. Add the cumin seeds and let their flavour infuse into the ghee for about 30 seconds, being careful not to burn the cumin. Stir in the garlic and fry for about 2 minutes, again being careful not to burn the garlic. Add the chopped curry leaves and bird's eye chillies and fry for further 30 seconds.

Pour in 375ml (1½ cups) water, add the salt and chilli flakes and bring to a simmer. Slowly add the semolina while stirring continuously. Make sure no lumps form as the semolina thickens in the water. Continue simmering until you have a dough that is about the same consistency as mashed potatoes. Remove from the heat to cool.

Once cooled, knead the semolina dough for a couple of minutes, then add the grated potato and knead for a few minutes more until you have a soft but workable dough. Take a ball of the dough that is just larger than a golf ball and dust it with the flour, then roll it out into a circle about 20cm (8in) in diameter. You could use a round cutter to make perfect circles, but I rarely do this. Repeat with the rest of the dough. Brush each paratha generously with melted ghee.

When ready to cook, place a frying pan or tawa over a high heat and cook the parathas until lightly browned on both sides, about 2 minutes per side. I usually brush the parathas with melted ghee as they cook. Repeat with the remaining parathas. Serve hot topped with the chopped red onion, if using.

GRILLED NAANS
MAKES 6

This is an classic naan recipe and my preferred dough for the curry-filled naans on page 119. It's a great naan recipe, but if you want to make naans more quickly, try the dough I use for my karahi naans on page 153. I've been making this dough for over 20 years and though I don't make it as often as the quicker version, it is still my favourite.

PREP TIME: 20 MINS, PLUS RISING TIME
COOKING TIME: 20 MINS

500g (4 cups) plain (all-purpose) flour, plus extra for dusting
½ tbsp salt
1 tbsp baking powder
150ml (⅔ cup) full-fat (whole) milk
7g (2½ tsp) fast-action dried yeast
2 tbsp sugar
2 eggs
135g (generous ½ cup) Greek yoghurt
Oil, for greasing
3 tbsp melted ghee
Nigella seeds (black onion seeds), for sprinkling

Sift the flour, salt and baking powder into a large bowl. Warm the milk in the microwave or in a small pan on the hob until hand-hot. Pour into a jug, add the yeast and sugar and whisk together. Cover with a cloth and leave in a warm place for about 20 minutes. It should foam up. If it doesn't, don't worry, your naans will still rise.

Lightly beat the eggs and yoghurt together. Pour the yeasty milk mixture into the flour, along with the whisked eggs and yoghurt, and mix everything to combine.

Tip the dough out onto a clean work surface and knead for about 10 minutes until you have a soft, slightly sticky ball of dough. Brush the insides of the bowl with a little oil and place the dough back in the bowl. Cover and leave to rise for 1 hour, or up to 24 hours – longer rising times achieve a better flavour.

Once risen, pull off a tennis-ball-sized chunk of dough and, using your hands or a rolling pin, roll it out on a lightly floured work surface into a flat, circular disc or teardrop shape, about 5mm (¼in) thick. Slap the disc between your hands to remove the excess flour.

Heat a dry frying pan over a high heat and, when very hot, place the naan in it. It will begin to cook on the underside then bubble on the top. Check the bottom regularly to ensure it doesn't burn. If it begins to get too dark, turn the naan over to get a bit of colour on the other side. Each naan should take no more than 3–5 minutes to cook. This can also be done on a lightly greased grill with no pan.

Transfer the cooked naan to a plate, brush with a little ghee and sprinkle with nigella seeds. Keep warm while you cook the remaining dough in the same way.

KARAHI NAANS
MAKES 6

The dough for this recipe is made curry-house style – that means you can make the dough and cook them straight away, though letting the dough sit is better if you can. You might have heard of or even tried to make naans in a pan on the hob. Here cooking on an upside down karahi over a hot fire gets even better results and it offers a quick way to cook lots of naans at once. You can see another photograph of these karahi naans being cooked on page 57.

PREP TIME: 25 MINS
COOKING TIME: 10 MINS

250ml (1 cup) warm full-fat (whole) milk
Approx. 150ml (generous ½ cup) warm water
2 eggs, lightly beaten
1 tsp salt
3 heaped tbsp caster (superfine) sugar
1 tbsp nigella seeds (black onion seeds)
500g (4 cups) self-raising (self-rising) flour, sifted, plus extra as needed
70ml (¼ cup) rapeseed (canola) oil
Melted ghee or butter, for brushing
3 tbsp finely chopped coriander (cilantro)

Pour the milk and water into a large mixing bowl. Add the eggs, salt, sugar and nigella seeds and whisk well. Start adding in the flour, whisking as you do. Once you've added all the flour, the mixture will still look very soupy and far too wet to work into dough balls. I recommend covering the dough with a wet cloth and letting it sit for at least 3 hours, or overnight for best results. That said, you could just jump right into finishing the recipe at this stage.

When ready to make the naans, slowly start adding more flour. The idea here is to add enough flour so that the dough is workable; you will need quite a lot. The dough should be very soft and slightly sticky, but not so sticky that it sticks to your hands. If it does, dust with a little bit more flour until you can easily divide and form the dough into 6 spongy dough balls.

Once the dough balls are formed, you could let them sit, covered, for about 30 minutes or up to 24 hours, but again, you can also push forward and make the naans immediately. As the dough is so soft, you shouldn't need a rolling pin. Dip your fingers in the oil and start patting the first dough ball to flatten it. Continue patting it and forming it into a disc until it is flat. Repeat with the remaining dough balls.

To cook, prepare a direct heat fire (see page 10). Pick up one of the flattened naans, with the oiled side flat on your hand. Dip your other hand in water and dampen the other side of the naan and then slap it hard onto the bottom of an upturned karahi or wok. Repeat with the remaining naans.

Place the karahi with all the naans on it over the fire. As the karahi heats up, it will begin cooking the naans and big bubbles will appear on top. Once you are happy with the way your bubbly naans look (mine usually bubble up to perfection in about 5 minutes), pick the karahi up with a couple of towels and turn the naans towards the fire to char. Remove the naans with a metal spatula or knife and brush with the melted ghee or butter. Sprinkle with the chopped coriander (cilantro) before serving.

PERFECT GRILLED ROTIS
MAKES 10

Here's a quick lesson for you. Hold your hands in fists in front of you as if you are holding a rolling pin. Now move your hands in small clockwise circles. This is the technique you need to master to make perfect rotis and chapatis. If you just go back and forth with a rolling pin, it will be very difficult to make them round and evenly flat. This will take some practice, though, so below I have explained another rolling option for beginners.

PREP TIME: 15 MINS, PLUS RESTING TIME
COOKING TIME: 10 MINS

250g (2 cups) maida or plain (all purpose) flour, plus extra for dusting
1 tsp salt
Melted ghee, for brushing (optional)

Sift the flour and salt into a mixing bowl, add 125ml (½ cup) water and start working it into the flour. It will become crumbly. Slowly add about 125ml (½ cup) more water a few drops at a time while kneading until you have a soft dough. Transfer to a clean surface and knead for about 10 minutes, adding a little more water if the dough is looking dry. You want to end up with a smooth, soft dough that when pressed with a finger has some resistance but leaves a good indentation mark. Cover the bowl with a damp cloth and leave to rest for 30 minutes.

After 30 minutes, tip the dough out and knead again for 3 minutes. Roll into a sausage and divide it into 10 equal-sized pieces. Take one dough ball and dust it liberally with flour. Roll it with your hands into a perfect ball and then press it down to flatten it a little. There should be no cracks. If it cracks at the edges, work it into a ball again and knead further before rolling and flattening once more. Repeat with the remaining dough balls, keeping them covered so that they don't dry out.

To roll out the discs, try using the method described above to create rotis about 20cm (8in) in diameter and 2mm (1/16in) thick; otherwise roll them out as best you can. Stack the finished rotis on a plate – they won't stick together – and cover.

To cook, prepare a direct heat fire (see page 10). Place a frying pan or tawa over the hottest part of the fire and, when hot, place a roti in the pan and cook for about 10 seconds. Flip it over and cook the other side for about 30 seconds, or until it starts to brown. While the roti is cooking, use tongs or a flat spatula to flatten it. Flip the roti again to cook for a further 10 seconds, then take it out of the pan and place it on the cooking grate right over the flame. It should puff up, but this takes practice, so don't worry if it doesn't. Flip a few more times then transfer to a plate. Keep warm while you cook the remaining rotis. I like to brush the hot rotis with melted ghee before serving.

RAJASTHANI KHOBA ROTI

MAKES 4–8

I love cooking these unique Rajasthani rotis on the barbecue. Brushed with melted ghee while still hot, they're amazing! They might look difficult to make with all those nooks and crannies, but they really aren't. Although usually dunked into a good curry, these rotis are also delicious served with dhal (see page 145), too.

PREP TIME: 25 MINS
COOKING TIME: 5 MINS

500g (4 cups) chapati or wholemeal (whole wheat) flour
2 tsp salt
2 tbsp melted ghee, plus extra for brushing
2 tsp cumin seeds, toasted (optional)
3 garlic cloves, finely chopped (optional)
2 tbsp rapeseed (canola) oil, plus extra for greasing

Sift the flour and salt into a mixing bowl and add 1 tablespoon of the melted ghee, the cumin and garlic, if using, and the oil. Mix well with your hands. Now slowly add about 500ml (2 cups) water while kneading until you have a soft, easily workable ball of dough. Cover and leave to rest for 15 minutes.

Divide the dough into 4–8 balls. I like to make large khoba rotis, but you might prefer to make smaller ones, depending on the size of your pan. Roll out the dough balls into 1cm (½in) thick rotis.

Pinch the dough in the centre of the roti with your fingers and continue pinching outwards to create the indentations these rotis are famous for. Take your time to make this look good! Repeat until all the rotis are finished. (Once you get the hang of this technique, you can do it when the rotis are in the pan.)

When ready to cook, prepare a direct heat fire (see page 10). Place a lightly greased frying pan over the hottest part of the fire and when hot, put a roti in the pan with the pinched side facing up and cook for about 2 minutes. Flip it over and cook the pinched side for a further 2 minutes. It should now be cooked through, but if not, flip it over again and cook until it is.

To finish, take the roti out of the pan and place it, pinched side down, directly on the grill over the fire to char just a little. Be careful: if your fire is too hot, it will quickly burn. Brush with plenty of ghee and keep warm. Repeat with the remaining rotis.

TRUFFLE AND PECORINO KULCHAS
MAKES 8

Kulchas are similar to naans, but unlike naans, they are unleavened. The idea for truffle and pecorino kulchas comes from my friends at Pataka in London. I'm telling you, this recipe is amazing. I make them all the time now. You can cook these kulchas using any of the cooking methods for breads in this book. I like to grill them on the cooking grate right over the fire.

PREP TIME: 25 MINS
COOKING TIME: 30 MINS

FOR THE KULCHA DOUGH
500g (4 cups) plain (all-purpose) flour
1 tsp salt
2 tsp baking powder
1 tbsp rapeseed (canola) oil
100ml (scant ½ cup) full-fat (whole) milk
2½ tsp sugar
1 egg, lightly beaten

FOR THE FILLING
4 tbsp rapeseed (canola) oil
1 tsp cumin seeds
250g (9oz) button mushrooms, finely chopped
250g (9oz) shiitake mushrooms, finely chopped
50g (2oz) mozzarella, grated
75g Cheddar cheese, grated
100g (3½oz) pecorino cheese, grated
2 tbsp truffle oil, plus extra for drizzling
½ tbsp finely chopped ginger
2 green bird's eye chillies, finely chopped
2 tbsp finely chopped coriander (cilantro)
Salt, to taste

TO SERVE
½ tsp shiitake mushroom powder (optional)

In a large bowl, combine all the ingredients for the dough with 100ml (scant ½ cup) water and bring together to form a soft dough. Tip onto a clean surface and knead for at least 5 minutes. It should be easy to knead and not sticking to your hands, so add a little more flour if needed. Return the dough to the bowl and cover with a moist cloth while you prepare the filling.

To make the mushroom filling, heat the oil in a frying pan over a medium-high heat. When hot, add the cumin seeds and fry for about 30 seconds, then stir in the chopped mushrooms. Season with salt and cook until the mushrooms are golden brown, about 15 minutes. Transfer this mushroom mixture to a plate lined with paper towels to soak up any excess oil.

Divide the dough into 8 equal-sized dough balls, keeping them covered with the cloth while you work.

Combine the mushrooms with the remaining filling ingredients. Divide into 8 equal-sized balls, then take one of the dough balls, make a deep indentation in it with your thumb and place one of the filling balls in it. Bring the dough around the filling so that it is completely enclosed. Repeat with the remaining dough and filling balls.

When ready to cook, prepare a direct heat fire (see page 10). Lightly brush the cooking grate with oil. Roll out the dough balls into flat rounds that are about 5mm (¼in) thick. Brush each kulcha lightly with truffle oil and place on the grill. Depending on the size of your grill, you might need to do this in batches. Cook on one side until lightly browned, about 1–2 minutes, then flip over to cook the other side for another couple of minutes. The kulchas will puff up, which is what makes them so light and delicious. Transfer to a plate, sprinkle with a little shiitake mushroom powder, if using, and drizzle with more truffle oil. Keep warm under a clean tea (dish) towel while you cook the remaining kulchas.

Top: Truffle and pecorino kulchas
Bottom: Rajasthani khoba roti (page 155)

TANDOORI COFFEE
SERVES 2

The first time I saw this done, I couldn't believe what I was seeing. My friend Jomon Kuriakose took my wife and me to a tandoori coffee stall in Cochin and it was a real show. The coffee was amazing and, being a bit of a coffee snob, I was surprised to learn that it was actually made with instant coffee. Pouring the coffee mixture into clay chai cups right out of the tandoor makes the prepared coffee mixture boil over and really adds to the flavour (see photograph opposite). You can heat the cups up in the coals of a tandoor, a covered barbecue or simply place them in the coals of a campfire.

PREP TIME: 10 MINS
COOKING TIME: 10 MINS

500ml (2 cups) full-fat (whole) milk
2 tbsp good-quality instant coffee (more or less to taste)
Sugar, to taste (optional)

Prepare a direct heat fire (see page 10). Place two clay chai cups on the coals and let them heat up until fiery hot. Meanwhile, pour the milk and 250ml (1 cup) water into a saucepan and bring to a boil on the cooking grate over the coals. When it comes to a boil, take it off the high heat and place it over a cooler part of the fire to keep warm. Stir in the instant coffee and sugar, if using, until fully combined.

Using tongs, pick up one of the chai cups and place it in a saucepan, preferably with a spout. Fill the cup with half of the coffee mixture. The coffee will bubble over like a geyser into the pan. Use your tongs to pick the chai cup up and pour any remaining coffee into the pan.

Pour the coffee into a coffee cup to serve and repeat with the remaining coffee and chai cup.

TANDOORI CHAI
SERVES 2

It was only after learning about tandoori coffee that I discovered that tandoori chai is also hugely popular. My wife loves this smoky tea. You just need a couple of clay chai cups and you can serve something amazing at the end of your barbecue feast. Both this and the tandoori coffee recipe can be easily scaled up to serve a crowd.

PREP TIME: 10 MINS
COOKING TIME: 10 MINS

2.5cm (1in) piece of ginger, roughly chopped
3 green cardamom pods
1 lemongrass stalk, roughly chopped
500ml (2 cups) full-fat (whole) milk
3 tsp loose-leaf black tea
Sugar, to taste

Prepare a direct heat fire (see page 10). Place two clay chai cups on the coals and let them heat up until fiery hot. Meanwhile, put the ginger, cardamom pods and lemongrass in a pestle and mortar and pound a few times to break them down a bit. Pour the milk and 175ml (¾ cup) water into a saucepan along with the tea, sugar and pounded ingredients and bring to a boil on the cooking grate over the coals. Remove from the heat once boiled and allow to steep for a couple of minutes.

Using tongs, pick up one of the chai cups and place it in a saucepan, preferably with a spout. Strain half of the tea through a tea strainer directly into the hot chai cup. It will bubble over into the pan. Use your tongs to pour out any tea that remains in the chai cup, then pour into a clean cup to serve. Repeat with the remaining tea.

FLAVOURSOME EXTRAS

We all love a good sauce or two to go with our barbecued meals. Here are some of my favourites, as well as a few marinades and spice rubs that you can use on pretty much everything. For that matter, you can use all the marinades in this book as you wish. Just because I used my cafreal marinade for the chicken wings on page 14, doesn't mean you're limited to that. Use the marinade for chicken or lamb tikka if you like! You can decide where and how to use any of the recipes.

ROASTED ONION RAITA

MAKES APPROX. 500ML (2 CUPS)

If you're cooking on the barbecue, you might as well make this simple but delicious raita to go with your meal. It is slightly smoky, with the onions becoming naturally sweet when cooked in the embers this way.

PREP TIME: 10 MINS
COOKING TIME: 1 HOUR

2 onions, unpeeled
1 tsp cumin seeds
½ cucumber, grated (remove the seeds from the core if you have time)
250g (1 cup) Greek yoghurt
1 tbsp finely chopped coriander (cilantro)
Juice of ½ lemon (more or less to taste)
Salt, to taste
Milk, for thinning the raita (optional)

Prepare a charcoal or wood fire. When the embers are ashed over and hot, place the 2 whole onions right down in them and leave to cook for 1 hour, moving them around from time to time, until the onions are really soft and the skins are blackened.

While the onions are cooking, place a dry frying pan onto the embers or on the cooking grate. When hot, add the cumin seeds and toast until fragrant and warm to the touch, about 30 seconds. Be careful not to burn the seeds or they will turn bitter. Transfer the toasted seeds to a bowl to cool.

When the onions are cooked, remove the skins and chop the flesh, roughly or finely depending on your preference. Pour the chopped onions into the bowl with the cumin seeds and add the remaining ingredients. Stir well to combine. If you prefer a thinner raita, add a drop or two of milk.

This will keep, covered in the fridge, for about 3 days.

MINT SAUCE

MAKES APPROX. 250ML (1 CUP)

Mint sauce is a favourite at Indian restaurants and takeaways and there are many different recipes. More often than not, the sauce is quite thin and that is how I have made the recipe below, but you could make it thicker by leaving out the milk. The most important thing is to make it taste just like you want it to, so test and experiment by adding more or less of the ingredients and you'll find exactly what you are looking for.

PREP TIME: 10 MINS

200g (generous ¾ cup) Greek yoghurt
1 tbsp shop-bought mint sauce (I use Coleman's)
½ tsp sugar
½ tsp cumin seeds
¼ tsp Kashmiri chilli powder
1 garlic clove, very finely chopped
Juice of 1 lemon
Milk, for thinning the sauce (optional)
Salt, to taste
Green food colouring (optional)

Put the yoghurt in a mixing bowl and whisk until smooth. Whisk in the mint sauce, then add the sugar, cumin seeds, chilli powder, chopped garlic and lemon juice. If you prefer a thinner consistency, add a drop or two of milk. Season with salt and add a little green food colouring if you want the sauce to be as green as it is at many restaurants.

This will keep, covered in the fridge, for about 3 days.

RED CHILLI SAUCE
MAKES 250ML (1 CUP)

The perfect accompaniment for samosas, papadams and, well, most things really! This dip is like the one you get when you order papadams at a curry house and it's really easy to make. Lately I've been making it with sriracha, but a more traditional version would use a sweet Indian chilli sauce. Although you could easily prepare this on the grill, I usually just prepare it in my kitchen.

PREP TIME: 5 MINS
COOKING TIME: 25 MINS

2 tbsp rapeseed (canola) oil
½ tsp black mustard seeds
½ tsp cumin seeds
¼ tsp nigella seeds (black onion seeds)
1 star anise
3 garlic cloves, minced
70ml (¼ cup) sweet chilli sauce or sriracha
2 tbsp ketchup
½ tsp Kashmiri chilli powder (more or less to taste)
½ tsp red food colouring (optional)
½ tsp dried fenugreek leaves (kasoori methi)
Juice of ½ lemon (more or less to taste)
Salt, to taste

Heat the oil in a large frying pan over a medium-high heat and when visibly hot, stir in the mustard seeds. When they begin to crackle, stir in the cumin seeds, nigella seeds and star anise and move them around in the oil for about 20 seconds. Stir in the minced garlic and fry for about 30 seconds, then add 125ml (½ cup) water and the sweet chilli sauce or sriracha, ketchup, chilli powder and the red food colouring, if using. I add about ½ teaspoon, but add as much or as little as you like as the colouring adds no real flavour.

To finish, add the dried fenugreek leaves (kasoori methi) by rubbing them between your fingers, then season with salt and lemon juice to taste.

Allow to cool and then pour into a sterilized jar with a tight-fitting lid (see page 166). This will keep in the fridge for several weeks.

GREEN CHUTNEY
MAKES ABOUT 400ML (1½ CUPS)

This is exactly as titled – a green chutney. Below I have provided my 'go to' recipe, but feel free to vary it. It's green, of course, because of the coriander (cilantro) and mint leaves along with the chillies. You can adjust this herb chutney to include just coriander, just mint or a combination of the two; for example, for many recipes I prefer a strong coriander chutney whereas with others, like lamb kebabs, I like some mint thrown in. The amount of yoghurt you use can also be adjusted. However you make this, I promise it will be delicious.

PREP TIME: 10 MINS

60g (2 packed cups) coriander (cilantro) or mint leaves, or a mixture of both
6 green bird's eye chillies, roughly chopped
Juice of 1 lime
½ tsp cumin seeds (optional)
200g (generous ¾ cup) Greek yoghurt, taste (optional)
Salt, to taste

Using a spice grinder or small food processor, blend the herbs, chillies and lime juice to a thick, smooth paste. Add a little water if needed.

Transfer the paste to a small bowl, add the cumin seeds, if using, and then begin whisking in the yoghurt a little at a time. The more you add, the paler and less intense your chutney will become. Colour isn't as important as flavour, though, so whisk the yoghurt in until you are happy with how it tastes, or leave it out for a more intense flavour. Season with salt then chill until needed.

This will keep, covered in the fridge, for about 3 days.

Clockwise from top left: Red chilli sauce; mint sauce (page 161); green chutney; roasted onion raita (page 161); homemade papads (page 13)

SPICY TOMATO CHUTNEY
MAKES 500ML (2 CUPS)

I must make this at least once a week. It's good on almost everything, from papadams to kebabs to omelettes. You can make this chunky or smooth depending on what you prefer. I like it not quite chunky but not super smooth either. If you prefer it really chunky, I suggest using fresh tomatoes with the pulp removed and then finely chopped. I prefer to use tinned (canned) as it's easier and gets the colour I'm looking for.

PREP TIME: 10 MINS

400g (14oz) tinned (canned) chopped
    tomatoes
1 onion, finely chopped
2 garlic cloves, finely chopped
3–6 green bird's eye chillies, finely chopped
Small handful of chopped coriander (cilantro)
Juice of 1 lime
Salt, to taste

Put the tomatoes, chopped onion, garlic, bird's eye chillies and coriander (cilantro) into a blender or food processor and blend to your desired consistency. Squeeze in the lime juice and season with salt. The salt is important here – I use quite a lot as it really brings out the flavours of the other ingredients.

This will keep, covered in the fridge, for about 3 days.

KASHMIRI HOT SAUCE
MAKES 500ML (2 CUPS)

At my cooking classes, the food we make is always accompanied by different hot sauces and chutneys. I am often asked how I make my hot sauces and the answer is that I make them with chilli powders and also fresh chillies. Although I have used Kashmiri chilli powder for this recipe, feel free to experiment with other chilli powders or fresh red chillies. The key to getting the flavour right is tasting it and adjusting the sour (vinegar), spicy (chilli powder) and savoury (salt) flavours to your own preference.

PREP TIME: 10 MINS

60g (2¼oz) Kashmiri chilli powder
250ml (1 cup) distilled white, white wine
    or cider vinegar
1 tsp paprika (optional)
1 tsp cumin (optional)
1 tsp salt

Put all the ingredients into a blender with 250ml (1 cup) water and blend until smooth. Taste your creation, adding salt to taste and adjusting with more chilli powder, vinegar and/or water.

Pour into a sterilized jar (see page 166) with a tight-fitting lid. This will keep for several months (and actually improves with age).

NOTE
Other ingredients can be added to this hot sauce, too. Try blending in some garlic powder, onion powder or dried herbs. Ground spices such as cumin, coriander, paprika and black pepper are also nice.

KEBAB-SHOP GARLIC SAUCE

MAKES 500ML (2 CUPS)

There are many recipes for the white garlic sauce that we all love to squirt over our kebabs, but they are all quite similar. Some sauces have 1 or 2 tablespoons of tahini paste in the mix, but that is more usual at Middle Eastern kebab restaurants than at Indian places. Different dried or fresh herbs are also often included and these should be added to taste, if using. Below is my recipe for garlic sauce, just how I like it.

PREP TIME: 5 MINS

230g (scant 1 cup) Greek yoghurt
230g (scant 1 cup) mayonnaise
½ tsp ground black pepper
4 garlic cloves, very finely chopped
1 tsp dried dill (optional)
1 tsp dried parsley (optional)
Juice of 1 lemon
Salt, to taste

Put the yoghurt and mayonnaise in a bowl and whisk until smooth. Add the remaining ingredients and season to taste with salt.

Store in the fridge in a jar with a tight-fitting lid or squeezy bottle until needed; it will keep for about 1 week.

KEBAB-SHOP RED CHILLI SAUCE

MAKES 400ML (1¾ CUPS)

Personally, I like my red chilli sauce a lot spicier than the following recipe, but this is about the heat you can expect at most establishments. If you don't like your sauce too hot, remove the seeds from the chillies. I leave them in and add about 10 more chillies!

PREP TIME: 5 MINS

3 red bird's eye chillies, roughly chopped
400g (14oz) tinned (canned) chopped
    tomatoes
3–4 garlic cloves, crushed
1 tbsp tomato purée (see page 169)
½ tsp ground black pepper
Juice of 1 lemon or 1 tbsp white vinegar
Salt, to taste

Put all the ingredients except the salt in a blender or food processor and blend until smooth. Taste and season with salt.

Store in the fridge in a jar with a tight-fitting lid or squeezy bottle until needed; it will keep for about 1 week.

GF <30

MY ALL-PURPOSE BBQ SAUCE
MAKES 1.5 LITRES (6 CUPS)

I have been making this barbecue sauce for three decades. The original recipe ticked all the boxes, so I never saw the need to change it. While writing this book, however, I decided to move away from my comfort zone a bit and did just that. Good news is, I was very happy with the results. This barbecue sauce is used in a few recipes in this book, but I bet you can find a few more uses for it. The Dijon mustard, Worcestershire sauce and molasses don't feature in any Indian recipes I've seen, but I like them so in they went!

PREP TIME: 15 MINS
COOKING TIME: 15 MINS

70ml (¼ cup) rapeseed (canola) oil
1 tsp black mustard seeds
1 tsp cumin seeds
30 fresh or frozen curry leaves
2 onions, very finely chopped
1 red (bell) pepper, very finely chopped
½ tsp salt, plus extra to taste
3 green bird's eye chillies, finely chopped (more or less to taste)
4 garlic cloves, crushed and finely chopped
2.5cm (1in) piece of ginger, peeled and finely chopped
800g (1lb 12oz) tinned (canned) plum tomatoes
70ml (¼ cup) Dijon mustard (optional)
200ml (generous ¾ cup) Worcestershire sauce
70ml (¼ cup) hot sauce (I use Frank's RedHot brand)
3 tbsp tamarind paste
70ml (¼ cup) molasses
100g (3½oz) dark brown sugar
70ml (¼ cup) cider vinegar
1 tbsp chilli powder (more or less to taste)
1 tbsp ground cumin
1 tsp ground coriander
½ tsp ground allspice
15g (1 cup) chopped coriander (cilantro), leaves and stalks
Freshly ground black pepper, to taste

Heat the oil in a saucepan over a medium-high heat. When visibly hot, add the black mustard seeds. When they begin to pop, add the cumin seeds and curry leaves. Swirl it all around in the oil and then add the chopped onions and red (bell) pepper. Sprinkle with the salt and fry, stirring regularly, for about 7 minutes, or until the onion is soft and lightly golden in colour. Add the chillies, garlic and ginger and fry for a further minute. Add all the remaining ingredients along with 250ml (1 cup) water and simmer for 15 minutes.

Taste the sauce and adjust the seasoning. It should be sweet, sour and a little spicy. Make the recipe your own by adding more of the sour, sweet and spicy ingredients if you like. Just be sure to keep them balanced.

Pour into a sterilized jar with a tight-fitting lid and keep in the fridge until ready to use. This sauce will keep for about a month.

SPICY VERSION
Throw in a few minced habanero chillies for more heat. These not only spice it up but also add an amazing flavour.

NOTE ON STERILIZING JARS
To sterilize jars, preheat the oven to 110°C (225°F/Gas ¼). If your jars have rubber sealing rings on the lid, remove them and boil in water for 5 minutes. Wash the jars thoroughly in hot, soapy water and rinse well, then place on a baking tray in the preheated oven for about 15 minutes until dry. Carefully remove them from the oven and fill them while still hot.

TAMARIND SAUCE/ MARINADE

MAKES 250ML (1 CUP)

This is a great tangy, sweet and mildly spiced sauce that is delicious as a dip or marinade. As a marinade, it can be brushed over meats like chicken and duck (see page 58) or fish such as tuna. Once you try it, I think you'll find many other uses for it.

PREP TIME: 10 MINS
COOKING TIME: 15 MINS

200g (7oz) block tamarind
1 tsp ground cumin
1 tsp chaat masala (see page 168)
½ tsp ground ginger
1 tsp Kashmiri chilli powder
1 tbsp light brown sugar or grated jaggery
Salt, to taste

Break the tamarind into a saucepan and cover with 375ml (1½ cups) water. Bring to a simmer over a medium-high heat and simmer for 5 minutes. Take off the heat and let sit for 5 more minutes.

Using a wooden spoon or potato masher, mash the tamarind into the water. The sauce will thicken to the consistency of ketchup. Strain this through a sieve into a mixing bowl, pushing the solids through. Discard any solids that remain in the sieve. Return the tamarind sauce to the saucepan and add the cumin, chaat masala, ground ginger, chilli powder and sugar. Simmer for about 3 minutes, or until all the sugar has dissolved. Add a drop more water if the sauce is becoming too thick or cook it down if it is too thin. Taste the sauce and season with salt or more sugar and chilli powder if needed. If you add more sugar, make sure you cook it again until the sugar has completely dissolved, adding more water if needed.

Allow to cool and then pour into a sterilized jar (see page 166). This can be stored in the fridge for several weeks. Keep in the fridge until ready to use.

TANDOORI MASALA

MAKES 120G (1¼ CUPS)

There are a lot of commercial tandoori masalas out there but this homemade version will get you superior results. You can make a delicious tandoori marinade for meat, seafood and vegetables by simply whisking this tandoori masala with Greek yoghurt to taste. You could also whisk it with a little lemon juice and rapeseed (canola) oil for a dairy-free marinade.

Mildly spiced and sour tandoori masala is also great stirred into some curries, such as the tikka masala curry sauce on page 134. Go ahead and experiment; if it sounds like it would be good stirred into a sauce, it probably will be.

PREP TIME: 8 MINS
COOKING TIME: 2 MINS

3 tbsp coriander seeds
3 tbsp cumin seeds
1 tbsp black mustard seeds
5cm (2in) cinnamon stick or cassia bark
Small piece of mace
3 dried Indian bay leaves (cassia leaves)
1 tbsp ground ginger
2 tbsp garlic powder
2 tbsp dried onion powder
2 tbsp amchoor (dried mango powder)
1 tbsp (or more) red food colouring powder (optional)

Roast the whole spices in a dry frying pan over a medium-high heat until warm to the touch and fragrant, moving them around the pan as they roast and being careful not to burn them. If they begin to smoke, take them off the heat. Tip onto a plate to cool.

Grind to a fine powder in a spice grinder or pestle and mortar and tip into a bowl. Stir in the ground ginger, garlic powder, onion powder and amchoor (dried mango powder).

Stir in the red food colouring powder, if using. Store in an air-tight container in a cool, dry place and use within 2 months.

CHAAT MASALA
MAKES APPROX. 4 TABLESPOONS

If I know I'm going to be using a lot of chaat masala, I double or triple this recipe. Usually, chaat masala is used in small amounts so this is how I tend to make it. You can buy good-quality chaat masala in Asian shops but this homemade version takes it all up a notch.

PREP TIME: 5 MINS
COOKING TIME: 2 MINS

1 tbsp coriander seeds
1 tbsp cumin seeds
2 tsp amchoor (dried mango powder)
1 tsp garam masala (see right)
1 tbsp ground black salt
1 tsp freshly ground black pepper

Toast the coriander and cumin seeds in a dry frying pan over a medium heat until warm to the touch and fragrant but not yet smoking. Tip into a spice grinder or pestle and mortar with the remaining ingredients and grind to a fine powder.

This will keep for up to 2 months in an air-tight container with little loss of flavour but it is best used on the day you make it.

GARAM MASALA
MAKES APPROX. 4 TABLESPOONS

In the Indian subcontinent, garam masala is made daily to enhance and add flavour to a variety of different foods. My other books feature recipes for garam masala that make large amounts so that you can always have it on hand when needed. The thing is, garam masala is best prepared and used on the day it is made. So here is a small batch of garam masala for you. You can always scale up the ingredients should you wish to make more. If you have some shop-bought garam masala in your cupboard, smell it and compare it to the much more powerful flavour and aroma of your homemade version.

PREP TIME: 5 MINS

1 tbsp cumin seeds
1 tbsp coriander seeds
1 tsp black peppercorns
2 tsp fennel seeds
½ tsp cloves
2.5cm (1in) cinnamon stick
1 Indian bay leaf
1 blade mace
Seeds from 4 green cardamom pods

Put all the spices in a dry frying pan and toast for about a minute over a medium heat or until warm to the touch and fragrant. Do not allow the spices to smoke! If they are smoking, they're burning, so transfer to a plate immediately to cool. Once cooled, grind in a spice grinder to a fine powder. You can also use a pestle and mortar, but it will take longer.

Store in an air-tight container for up to 3 months.

ALL-PURPOSE RUB
MAKES 170G (1½ CUPS)

I have been making this all-purpose rub for as long as I can remember. It is good on so many things. Coat pork ribs with it, roast chicken, a rib of beef... this rub works on pretty much everything, but is best used for barbecuing rather than direct grilling.

PREP TIME: 10 MINS

4 tbsp paprika
4 tbsp salt
4 tbsp light brown sugar or grated jaggery
4 tbsp garlic powder
3 tbsp dried onion powder
2 tbsp Kashmiri chilli powder
2 tsp ground black pepper
1½ tsp ground cumin
1½ tsp ground coriander

Combine all the ingredients in a glass jar and mix well. Store in an air-tight container in a cool, dry place until ready to use – as long as you are using fresh spices, it will keep for up to 3 months.

GARLIC AND GINGER (AND CHILLI) PASTE

Many of the recipes in this book call for garlic and ginger paste. Some call for garlic, ginger and chilli paste. The method for making both is the same and the amount you blend is completely down to your requirements.

PREP TIME: 5 MINS

For **garlic and ginger paste**, simply blend equal amounts of peeled garlic cloves and ginger with a drop of water in a blender or spice grinder to make a paste.

To make **garlic, ginger and chilli paste**, blend the garlic and ginger as above, then add green bird's eye chillies to taste and blend again; start with a small amount and then taste and add more as required.

This will keep, covered in the fridge, for 3 days but can also be frozen; freeze in ice-cube trays to give you handy tablespoon-sized portions.

TOMATO PURÉE

Tomato purée is used in most of the BIR curries in this book. You could use plain passata (sieved tomatoes) but generally the amounts are too small to warrant opening up a jar so I have given you a couple of options wherever this is called for.

METHOD 1
MAKES 4 TABLESPOONS
PREP TIME: 2 MINS

1 tbsp concentrated tomato paste
4 tbsp water

Mix the ingredients together to form a thinner paste. This recipe can easily be scaled up or down; just keep to 1 part tomato paste to 3 parts water.

METHOD 2
MAKES 425ML (1¾ CUPS)
PREP TIME: 5 MINS

400g (14oz) tin (can) plum tomatoes
Concentrated tomato paste, to taste (optional)

Blend the plum tomatoes to make a smooth purée. For a deeper colour, add a little concentrated tomato paste.

SUPPLIERS

INGREDIENTS

SPICE KITCHEN ONLINE LTD
Spice Kitchen supplies excellent quality spices and has also begun producing the spice blends from my books, such as mixed powder, garam masala, tandoori masala and chaat masala. You can also order spice tins filled with whole spices or their own spice blends from around the world. **www.spicekitchenuk.com**

SPICES OF INDIA
In addition to groceries and spices, you will also find a fantastic range of Indian kitchen and tableware. **www.spicesofindia.co.uk**

SWALEDALE BUTCHERS
Writing this book was made so much easier and delicious using meat from Swaledale Butchers. They deliver top quality meat, fresh to your doorstep. **www.swaledale.co.uk**

BBQS & TANDOOR OVENS

WEBER
The Weber Kettle barbecue is a great and reasonably priced barbecue for both indirect and direct heat cooking. Not only is it perfect for cooking at home, it is also easy to pack up and take with you when camping. **www.weber.com**

THÜROS BARBECUES
If you love kebabs, you've got to check out Thüros Kebab Grills. I love mine. **www.thueros.com**

KAMADO JOE BARBECUES
Looking for a ceramic barbecue? I've tried many but the Kamado Joe is the one I love most! **https://kamadojoe.co.uk/**

KADAI FIREBOWLS
A firebowl and barbecue in one! Perfect for grilling and cooking curries with a range of accessories. **www.kadai.co.uk**

TRAEGER BARBECUES
Traeger barbecues use wood pellets to cook the food. You can set the preferred temperature and then let the Traeger do all the work. This is the perfect barbecue for easy indirect cooking. **www.traeger.com**

AQUAFORNO BARBECUES
The Aquaforno is a fantastic and highly versatile barbecue, perfect for home and camping. **www.aquaforno.com**

SIZZLE GRILLS
Sizzle Grills manufactures Argentine-style parillas and other fun cooking equipment for cooking outdoors over fire. **www.sizzlegrills.co.uk**

BABA CLAY OVENS
Cooking in a tandoor oven is a lot of fun and also easier than you might think. I have given detailed instructions on using a tandoor in the link on page 7. The outdoor tandoor I use at home is a Baba Clay. It's an excellent piece of kit! **https://www.babaclayoven.co.uk/**

CHARCOAL

BIG K
I highly recommend the top quality lumpwood charcoal, charcoal briquettes and kiln dried longs supplied by Big K! **www.bigkproducts.co.uk**

COOKWARE

BIRMINGHAM BALTI BOWL COMPANY
The perfect pan for cooking curries over fire or indoors! **www.thebirminghambaltibowlco.com**

THERMAPEN
When roasting and grilling, it's important to get the internal temperature of your meat right. For reliable thermometers visit **www.thermapen.co.uk**

TOTALLY BBQ
This is an excellent source for planchas, grill pans, fire starters and many cooking accessories. **www.tbbq.co.uk**

INDEX

ACKNOWLEDGMENTS

This book is dedicated to my friend Chris Rodbourne, who sadly lost his long and courageous fight with cancer in 2021. Chris worked tirelessly as a moderator for my Facebook group and his wit and positive outlook on life is missed by many. Thank you Chris. RIP my friend.

As always, it was a pleasure to work with everyone at Quadrille to produce this book. Thank you to Sarah Lavelle for commissioning the project and to my editor, Clare Sayer, for all her help with my words and for bringing this book together.

Thanks to Kris Kirkham, who has worked with me on every cookbook I've written, and food stylist Rosie Reynolds, for bringing my recipes to life in a way that only they can.

A special thank you to chef Jomon Kuriakose who has become a great friend over the years and has inspired me through his knowledge of authentic Indian cuisine.

A big thank you goes out to the moderators of my Facebook group, Tim Martin, Karen Bolan, Claire Rees, Anne-Marie Goodfellow, James Vaisey and Derek Turnbull. It has been an honour to work with you over the past couple of years. You have made it possible for me to keep the page going while spending so many hours writing. I owe you a lot!

Thank you to my agent Clare Hulton for all her support and for once again making things happen.

Thanks so much Matt and Chiyo Buckle for the use of your amazing property that is featured in many of the photos in this book. It was such an ideal and beautiful location for cooking over fire.

In order to make this book as good as it could possibly be, I turned to some of the best barbecue gurus I know. Thank you so much Marcus Bawdon, Jon Finch, Christian Stevenson and Dan 'The Smokin' Elk' Whittaker.

I would like to thank all you curry and barbecue fans out there for picking up this book. I appreciate it so much and hope you enjoy this new collection of recipes.

Publishing Director: Sarah Lavelle
Project Editor: Clare Sayer
Designer: Alicia House
Cover Design: Smith & Gilmour
Photographer: Kris Kirkham
Photography Assistant: Eyder Rosso Gonçalves
Food Stylist: Rosie Reynolds and Troy Willis
Food Stylist Assistant: Antonia Bellini
Props Stylist: Faye Wears
Head of Production: Stephen Lang
Production Controller: Nikolaus Ginelli

First published in 2022 by Quadrille, an imprint of Hardie Grant Publishing

Quadrille
52–54 Southwark Street,
London SE1 1UN
quadrille.com

Text © 2022 Dan Toombs
Photography © 2022 Kris Kirkham
Design and layout © 2022 Quadrille

Cataloguing-in-Publication Data. A catalogue record for this book is available from the British Library.

ISBN 9781787138070

Printed in China

In five short years Dan took The Curry Guy from an idea to a reliable brand. The recipes are all developed and tested in Dan's home kitchen. And they work. His bestselling first cookbook – *The Curry Guy* – and the 250,000 curry fans who visit his blog every month can testify to that fact.

Dan holds regular cooking classes in North Yorkshire. Dates and times can be found on his website: www.greatcurryrecipes.net

If you have any recipe questions you can contact Dan (@thecurryguy) on Twitter, Facebook or Instagram.

81 385 49 8